Praise for Perry Carpenter

"The best security behaviors are the ones you never think about, that get ingrained as habits and become part of who you are. Perry's exploration of security as a cultural force, created by processes and communications but separate from them, is a unique look into precisely that zone of our identity. By stepping away from our biases about what security looks like and focusing on what it practically does, this book invites us forward."
—Matt Wallaert, Behavioral Scientist and Author of *Start At The End: How to Build Products that Create Change*

"In my time advising companies on how to become more resilient to social engineering, I've always touted the importance of building a strong security culture. Perry Carpenter is one of the world's foremost experts in how to do just that. Security leaders and business executives would be wise to listen to his advice and implement his suggestions."
—Kevin Mitnick, Principal, Mitnick Security

"Perry has his finger on the pulse of security awareness culture and knows how to bring it to life. His real-world expert advice focuses on what is actionable and most essential for protecting your organization right now."
—Rachel Tobac, CEO of SocialProof Security and Friendly Hacker

"Perry Carpenter understands that cyber security takes both technology and human accountability. In this excellent new book, he is able to show how both must work together to keep our companies, institutions, and society safe and secure. You should find a number of best practices and insights in this timely book."
—John R. Childress, Chairman, PYXIS Culture Technologies

"Security culture is fundamental to organizational resilience, efficiency, and success. Perry Carpenter is one of the world's leading experts in this space, and he communicates his expertise in a way that is engaging and accessible for all."
—Dr Jessica Barker, co-CEO of Cygenta and Author of *Confident Cyber Security*

Praise for Kai Roer

Kai is a pioneer in security culture awareness, showing CISOs how to drive meaningful changes and move their organizations forward.
—Mirko Zorz, Editor in Chief, Help Net Security

Kai has been pioneering the concepts around security culture for more than a decade, and I've known him for that time as he's built, and sold up, his CLTRe concept. His knowledge on benchmarking a security culture is second to none.
—Dan Raywood, Cybersecurity journalist (former)

I have seen Kai Roer demonstrate his passion and sincere dedication to improving the security culture of organizations for many years. Kai providing guidance for executives to understand their role and responsibility for creating a secure business ecosystem, through using *The Security Culture Playbook*, is a brilliant idea!
—Rebecca Herold, CEO of The Privacy Professor consultancy, and Privacy & Security Brainiacs SaaS services

I am enthused to learn that Kai Roer has written a new book about security culture.

Kai Roer has taken his many years of cyber experience and combined those with a vested interest in cyber security. By using Kai's Security Culture Framework, I got a tool to address the human and cultural factors in our organization to improve the security maturity.

With clear, everyday examples and analogies to reveal social and cultural triggers that drive human behaviour he guided me through my work. I immediately saw the experience, knowledge, and interpersonal skills that he had for working with people. I most admire Kai for his humor, his determination to reach whatever goals he has put up, and his devotion to throw light on the less technical part of information security.
—Anne-Marie Eklund Löwinder, Founder of Amelsec AB, inducted into the Internet Hall of Fame, Member of the Royal Swedish Academy of Engineering Science

There is no one better placed to present expertise related to security culture than Kai. Further, developing a security culture within a given organization is the first line of defence, which makes this book essential reading.
—Raj Samani, McAfee Fellow, Chief Scientist

Kai Is the world leader on security culture helping organizations understand what culture they currently have, what culture they would like to have, and more importantly how to get there.

—Quentyn Taylor, Senior Director – Product, Information Security and Global Incident Response Canon Europe Middle East and Africa

For over a decade, Kai Roer has advised and guided security executives on leading teams and developing culture. His pragmatic approach, informed by psychology and backed by metrics, moves beyond the fluffy platitudes so often found in leadership books. If you are looking for where to begin or wondering what good looks like, Kai Roer's expertise lights the path.

—J. Wolfgang Goerlich, CISO

I was quite happy living with the knowledge that I had invented the phrase "Security Culture." Then I met Kai. He had been working on the concept for a couple of years already and went on to become the master of the subject. I am proud to have been on some of that journey with him and have followed and implemented his work at some of the most forward-thinking organizations on the planet.

—Shan Lee, CISO, Wise PLC, ex-Just Eat

Kai is a consummate professional cyber security risk adjudicator and educator; I have known Kai and worked with him for several years, and he is someone I implicitly trust in all settings.

—Bill Hagestad, Author of *21st Century Chinese Cyberwarfare* and several other books on China's use of computer systems as national strategic weapons. He advises NATO, the US Marine Corps and interfaces with the Chinese People's Liberation Army (PLA).

There is no such thing as a comprehensive cybersecurity posture without a security culture program. Carpenter and Roer provide executives with all the tools they need to help secure the frontline of defense — the human. With ransomware and novel social engineering techniques on the rise, there has never been a timelier moment for this book — it simply is the must-read cyber book of the year!

—Dr. Lydia Kostopoulos, SVP Emerging Tech Insights

Kai Roer is a person who has been at the forefront of Security Awareness for many years and as such is leading by example. From the early days of his Awareness model to his recent book successes, Kai has proven time and again through his experience in the field implementing his knowledge that he is a true leader in this field.

—Stuart Coulson, Director, HiddenText Ltd

The Security Culture Playbook

Perry Carpenter
Kai Roer

WILEY

Published by John Wiley & Sons, Inc., Hoboken, New Jersey.
Published simultaneously in Canada.

978-1-119-87523-9
978-1-119-87529-1 (ebk.)
978-1-119-87524-6 (ebk.)

Limit of Liability/Disclaimer of Warranty: The publisher and the author make no representations or warranties with respect to the accuracy or completeness of the contents of this work and specifically disclaim all warranties, including without limitation warranties of fitness for a particular purpose. No warranty may be created or extended by sales or promotional materials. The advice and strategies contained herein may not be suitable for every situation. This work is sold with the understanding that the publisher is not engaged in rendering legal, accounting, or other professional services. If professional assistance is required, the services of a competent professional person should be sought. Neither the publisher nor the author shall be liable for damages arising herefrom. The fact that an organization or Website is referred to in this work as a citation and/or a potential source of further information does not mean that the author or the publisher endorses the information the organization or Website may provide or recommendations it may make. Further, readers should be aware the Internet Websites listed in this work may have changed or disappeared between when this work was written and when it is read.

For general information on our other products and services or for technical support, please contact our Customer Care Department within the United States at (800) 762-2974, outside the United States at (317) 572-3993 or fax (317) 572-4002.

Wiley also publishes its books in a variety of electronic formats. Some content that appears in print may not be available in electronic formats. For more information about Wiley products, visit our web site at www.wiley.com.

Library of Congress Control Number: 2021952665

Trademarks: WILEY and the Wiley logo are trademarks or registered trademarks of John Wiley & Sons, Inc. and/or its affiliates, in the United States and other countries, and may not be used without written permission. All other trademarks are the property of their respective owners. John Wiley & Sons, Inc. is not associated with any product or vendor mentioned in this book.

Cover image: © Getty Images/gremlin
Cover design: Wiley

SKY10033344_030322

For the wonderful community of security awareness, behavior, and culture professionals around the world. You are an inspiration.
And for my family, Siobhan, Sage, and Aoibheann. Thank you making life crazy and wonderful!

—Perry Carpenter

I dedicate this book to all the amazing first-responders who continuously keep our society safe and secure without regard for their own life and health. Thank you!

—Kai Roer

About the Authors

Perry Carpenter, C|CISO, MSIA, currently serves as Chief Evangelist and Strategy Officer for KnowBe4, the world's most popular security awareness and simulated phishing platform.

Perry has been a recognized thought leader on security awareness and the human factors of security for well over a decade. His broad background makes him uniquely positioned to understand nuances of awareness, behavior, and culture strategies that can be elusive. Perry's security culture influence-related experiences span multiple pivotal roles: from being a general employee receiving awareness training; to being an awareness program manager running complex global programs; to being the primary market analyst advising security leaders about awareness trends, success practices, and vendor platforms; to now helping lead the efforts of the world's largest and most successful security awareness and simulated phishing platform. Perry draws from this experience, along with cutting-edge research in the fields of marketing, communication, behavior science, and organizational culture management to inform his perspectives and advice for creating security culture influence programs that are transformational.

Before joining KnowBe4, Perry led security awareness, security culture management, and anti-phishing behavior management research at Gartner Research (NYSE:IT), in addition to covering areas of IAM strategy, CISO Program Management mentoring, and Technology Service Provider success strategies. With a long career as a security professional and researcher, Carpenter has broad experience in North America and Europe, providing security consulting and advisory services for many of the world's best-known brands.

Perry's previous book, *Transformational Security Awareness: What Neuroscientists, Storytellers, and Marketers Can Teach Us About Driving Secure Behaviors* (Wiley, 2019) quickly gained a reputation as being the go-to book for security awareness professionals worldwide, and, in 2021, received the honor of being inducted into the Cybersecurity Canon Hall of Fame, a collection of "must-read books for all cybersecurity practitioners—be they from industry, government, or academia—where the content is timeless, genuinely represents an aspect of the community that is true and precise, reflects the highest quality and, if not read, will leave a hole in the cybersecurity professional's education that will make the practitioner incomplete." Institute for Cybersecurity & Digital Trust (2022).

Perry is also the creator and host of the popular *8th Layer Insights* podcast (8thlayerinsights.com), an immersive narrative nonfiction exploration into the intersection of cybersecurity and the human condition. His guest list is a who's who of voices from cybersecurity, behavior sciences, creators, and more.

Perry holds a Master of Science in Information Assurance (MSIA) from Norwich University in Vermont and is a Certified Chief Information Security Officer (C|CISO).

You can connect with Perry on LinkedIn at linkedin.com/in/ perrycarpenter.

Kai Roer currently serves as Chief Research Officer for KnowBe4, the world's most popular security awareness and simulated phishing platform.

Kai has been providing actionable advice founded on empirical evidence to public and private organizations around the world since the 1990s. His work over the past decades has focused on helping organizations understand what culture they currently have, what culture they would like to have, and more importantly, how to get there. Kai works with the information security community on a global stage to educate the importance and impact that security culture has.

In 2010, he created the Security Culture Framework (SCF), a framework and methodology to build and maintain security culture. Kai later gifted the SCF to the open-source community, and it evolved into several spin-offs, including the Cybersecurity Culture Framework by The European Union Agency for Cybersecurity (ENISA) in 2015. Kai has authored and co-authored several books on leadership and technology. His popular book *Build a Security Culture* (IT-Governance, 2015) is widely considered as the guiding resource on the topic of security culture.

Before joining KnowBe4, Kai founded the security culture measurement company, CLTRe (pronounced culture), the world's first SaaS-platform built to measure and manage an organization's security culture. This new ability to measure security culture made it possible for organizations worldwide to understand exactly where and how to improve their security. KnowBe4 acquired CLTRe in 2019. After which, Kai built KnowBe4 Research, the research arm of KnowBe4, where he leads a team of researchers dedicated to improving the knowledge and understanding of the human factors that influence security.

Recognized by many as a leading global authority on the topic of security culture, he has received several awards, including the Ron Knode Service Award by the Cloud Security Alliance CSA for his extensive volunteer work in the security community around the world. Thanks to his invaluable contributions to the industry and his unique background that combines leadership, communication, and technology, Kai is a popular keynote speaker and guest lecturer. He focuses on presenting complex challenges in easy-to-understand language. He is also a frequent guest on podcasts, radio, and TV, where he explains security in ways that resonate with non-security people.

When Kai is not working, he enjoys riding his motorcycles, spending time in the outdoors, and BBQing with his family and friends.

You can connect with Kai at www.linkedin.com/in/kairoer and twitter.com/kairoer.

Acknowledgments

Security culture is a fun and difficult topic to bring to the page. And taking on the challenge certainly comes with its own set of risks and rewards. I'd like to thank all the folks who believed in this project and decided to take the risk. These are people who don't get the benefit of having their names on the cover of this book, but who are absolutely key to any success I or this book will have.

First, this book was a team effort between Kai Roer and me. Even before Kai and I became coworkers at KnowBe4, I was a fan of Kai's work in the field of security culture. It has been an honor to write this book with you!

Second, I need to think the great folks at Wiley Publishing. This is my second book with Wiley, and I'm continually struck by the professionalism, expertise, and compassion that the team brings to each project. Thanks to John Sleeva, Pete Gaughan, and Archana Pragash for helping transform our ramblings into something worthy to be read. And a special thank you to Jim Minatel, my acquisitions editor at Wiley for both this book as well as my previous book,

Transformational Security Awareness. Thanks for believing in both of these projects! You are a true advocate for the community.

I'd also like to thank my wonderful colleagues at KnowBe4. You are a true family, a source of inspiration, and a much needed support system. Any success I have is only because of the support and encouragement you provide. Thanks to Stu Sjouwerman, Kevin Mitnick, Michael Williams, Tiffany Mortimer, Megan Stultz, Kathy Wattman, Greg Kras, Lars Letonoff, Krish Venkatraman, Joanna Huisman, Rosa Smoothers, Lydia Kotsiopoulos, Javvad Malik, Roger Grimes, James McQuiggan, Erich Kron, Jacqueline Jayne, Wieringa, Anna Collard, John Just, Winn Schwartau, Kayley Melton, Kendra Irimie, Courtney Orzechowski, Jim Shields, and Rob McCollum. You mean more to me than you'll ever know.

I'd be remiss if I didn't thank my podcast family at The Cyber-Wire for being such an enthusiastic home for my *8th Layer Insights* podcast. You took a chance on me when I had a big vision and no experience, and you've been nothing but supportive. To Peter Kilpe, Jennifer Eiben, Bennett Moe, and Elliott Peltzman. Thanks for your support, advice, and belief in me.

Lastly, I'd like to extend thanks to the security awareness community. There are too many of you to name individually. But, know that this book is for you. You are truly inspiring.

—Perry Carpenter

Sitting here writing in my RV, somewhere in the Norwegian winter landscape, I am grateful for the fact that we live in a world where technology allows us to work from almost anywhere, if we bring our mind, our computer, and some network connectivity along with us. Thank you to all innovators, inventors, and all technologists throughout history—you made this possible!

Writing a book is a huge undertaking. Academics I know liken the process of writing a book with that process of producing a PhD thesis: a lot of dedication, many edits, a fair share of frustration, and a strange combination of solitude when writing and socializing when moving through the editing stages. Thank you, Wiley, and editors Pete Gaughan, Jim Minatel, and Archana Pragash.

Likewise, my team at KnowBe4 Research has been instrumental in the research that supports the writing of this book. Thank you, Anita Eriksen, Thea Ulimoen, and Jacopo Paglia, for your dedication and hard work!

I want to thank my employer KnowBe4 for their continued support of my work and passion: security culture. This book would never have happened without their help both in terms of the time needed for writing, and the sharing of the data and research results used throughout this book. Thank you, KnowBe4 founder and CEO Stu Sjouwerman, and KnowBe4 Chief Marketing Officer Michael Williams for making it possible for me to write this book.

A lot of this book is based on work I have done over my career. Several people have been crucial to me and the process of developing my understanding of security culture, including Roar Thon, Lars Jørgen Kielland Haug, Tone Hoddø Bakås, Jane LeClair, and J. Wolfgang Goerlich. Another instrumental person has been the late Rune Ask, who spent a lot of time taking my early drafts of the Security Culture Framework and adapting them to follow the standard of ISO.

A special mention to my good friend, business associate, cofounder, and brilliantly smart Gregor Petrič who through patience and dedication developed my understanding of the social science underlying much of the work I do. I also want to thank my friend and co-founder Aimee Laycock for her dedication and passion towards the topic of security culture. My son, Leo, the light of my life, and finally, I want to thank my amazing wife, Karolina. We both know that I could not have ventured on this journey without your support!

—Kai Roer

Contents at a Glance

Contents

Introduction

We're here to put a dent in the universe. Otherwise, why else even be here?

Steve Jobs

So, you're interested in security culture. You are not alone. The use of the phrase "security culture" has been steadily increasing over the past few years as organizations seek to combat the ever-present, daily drip of data breaches.

Somehow, despite all the great advancements in security-related technologies, we are faced with a simple truth: Technology, alone, is not enough. It does not offer sufficient protection against breach. Cybercriminals inevitably find ways to bypass the technology by targeting vulnerable humans; or a malicious or negligent insider may know just the right "work around" to effectively nullify your defenses. That's a recipe for a bad day.

Security leaders and business executives are coming to recognize that it's time to pay close attention to a long-neglected layer within their security stack: the human layer. But, you may ask, doesn't that mean that we should be talking about security awareness? The answer is both yes and no. Awareness is definitely part of the answer, but, by definition, simple awareness can take you only so far. Heck, even the old G.I. Joe public service announcements got that right. If you remember, they ended with the tag line, "Now you know. And knowing is half the battle."

For far too long, organizations have fallen into the trap of equating security awareness (information sharing) efforts with behavior change.

> *For far too long, organizations have fallen into the trap of equating security awareness (information sharing) efforts with behavior change.*

We all know, however, that knowledge doesn't always change behavior. Tons of people will tell you that they know they should adopt better behavior patterns around what they eat, their financial habits, and more. So, in the same way that technology alone is not sufficient for protection, knowledge alone isn't the answer either.

To add an effective human layer of defense, we need to embrace what is commonly referred to as the ABCs of cybersecurity: awareness, behavior, and culture. That recognition is why we are seeing a surge in people using the phrase "security culture." But here's the thing: So many people are throwing around the phrase without actually knowing what it means. They know that a good security culture must be a positive thing, but there is no precision or general agreement about what a good security culture looks like or how to achieve this promised security culture goodness.

That creates a dilemma. Security culture becomes this thing that has a lot in common with Bigfoot, the Abominable Snowman, or the Loch Ness Monster. People swear that it exists, but they have a hard time producing anything other than the equivalent of fuzzy photos and rambling stories of how they once saw one. And that's why we wrote this book.

Security culture becomes this thing that has a lot in common with Bigfoot, the Abominable Snowman, or the Loch Ness Monster. People swear that it exists, but they have a hard time producing anything other than the equivalent of fuzzy photos and rambling stories of how they once saw one. And that's why we wrote this book.

We're here to make security culture something that is not only understandable, but also measurable and manageable so you can finally get a handle on how to effectively engage your human layer of security and reduce human risk in your organization.

So let's go on a journey together—a journey to unlock the mysteries of security culture. Your guides (the collective "we" that you've been seeing throughout this short introduction) are Perry Carpenter and Kai Roer. Between the two of us, we have over 35 years of experience studying and consulting on various aspects of security culture. Seriously, we won't bore you with our bios and CVs here. You can find those elsewhere in this book. Just know that you are in good (virtual) hands as we guide you through this journey.

The path awaits. Let's begin.

Perry Carpenter & Kai Roer

February, 2022

What Lies Ahead?

Our goal in writing this book is to add much-needed precision and guidance to the security culture conversation. We believe the security industry is at a tipping point where leaders are ready to accept that technology is not a panacea. There have been so many great advances in security-related technologies over the past few decades, but those advances are not stemming the tide of breaches. Yes, those advances made technology-dependent hacking much more difficult, but they created the unintended consequence that our people are now the primary target. As an industry, we've been so focused on (and enamored with) technology that we've ignored the human side of the equation.

As leaders now seek to build their human-layer defenses, it is important that they move quickly and effectively. We can't afford to get this wrong. As such, our focus over the next several chapters will be to add much needed clarity about security culture: what it is; what it comprises; how to measure its subcomponents; and how to shape those all-important security-related facets of your organizational culture.

Here's a quick breakdown of what's to come.

Part I: Foundation

Part I is all about building a foundational understanding of why security culture is a critical, *got-to-pay-attention-to-it-now* topic. We discuss the current issues with defining "security culture," offer some hints to an ultimate definition (yeah, you'll have to wait a bit before we spill the beans on that one), and why security culture is a board-level imperative. We'll also provide some tie-ins with Perry's earlier work, *Transformational Security Awareness: What Neuroscientists, Storytellers, and Marketers Can Teach Us About Driving Secure Behaviors*.

Part II: Exploration

Part II is all about exploration. We focus on giving concrete examples of what a strong security culture looks like and what the consequences of a poor security culture can be. We'll put organizational culture and security culture under a microscope and examine the various subcomponents we find. Along the way, we will throw in some concepts from sociology, organizational culture management, and a few other disciplines. You'll also gain valuable insights from culture experts outside of the cybersecurity domain.

Part 3: Transformation

Here is where the proverbial rubber meets the proverbial road. Part III is about doing the work. It's about transformation. We'll walk you through the Security Culture Framework, a process that Kai developed over 15 years ago for getting a handle on security culture so that it can be improved. Since its creation, this process has been adopted by organizations and governments around the world. And, because anything worth managing is worth measuring, we'll take a deep dive into how to scientifically measure security culture across seven dimensions, and we'll give an overview of the Security Culture Survey, a tool that Kai and his team created over a decade ago. Since that time, it's been honed into a finely tuned scientific instrument that's been used to collect and analyze the largest security-culture-related dataset on earth. We'll also discuss culture-related gotchas, sticking points, and more. In the last bit of Part III, you'll hear from a number of security experts as they discuss security culture, and we'll leave you with some valuable tools and insights that so you can immediately leverage everything from this book. You'll be able to discuss security culture with confidence, measure maturity, gain executive support, and more.

Reader Support for This Book

We've also created a resource site for this book where we'll upload new worksheets, research studies, and other useful security culture-related information. It's at SecurityCultureBook.com.

How to Contact the Publisher

If you believe you've found a mistake in this book, please bring it to our attention. At John Wiley & Sons, we understand how important it is to provide our customers with accurate content, but even with our best efforts an error may occur.

In order to submit your possible errata, please email it to our Customer Service Team at wileysupport@wiley.com with the subject line "Possible Book Errata Submission".

How to Contact the Authors

We appreciate your input and questions about this book! Connect with Perry or Kai on LinkedIn at www.linkedin.com/in/perrycarpenter and www.linkedin.com/in/kairoer.

Part I

Foundation

Welcome to the journey! In Part I, we introduce the concept of security culture, why it is important, and (most importantly), the fact that you can measure and improve your culture. There's a lot to cover, so let's get started. But even before you turn to the first page of Chapter 1, we think it's important to give you a definition of security culture.

Security Culture: The ideas, customs, and social behaviors of a group that influence its security.

1

Chapter 1
You Are *Here*

The greatest danger in times of turbulence is not the turbulence
—it is to act with yesterday's logic.

Peter Drucker

"Security culture" has become a hot topic of late. If you are a cyber-security or business leader, you've no doubt seen the term appear in online articles, security presentations, and even a few vendor pitches. It's become a buzzword (or buzz *phrase*, if you want to be picky) du jour. Unfortunately, most of the time it is little more than a phrase uttered with gravitas, but devoid of real meaning.

Security culture is often confused with security awareness, the implementation of security processes, or even the use of security tools by end users. That initial misidentification becomes even more confusing because each of those things can feed into, or become an artifact of, security culture—but they are not in and of themselves security culture. Security culture is something different, something unique that is undeserving of the confusion that all too often surrounds it. And you know that; otherwise, you wouldn't be reading this book.

Our purpose here is to add precision and clarity to the topic. And, although we could easily fill several hundred pages with great content about security culture, that's not what this book is about. This book, dear reader, is a no-nonsense, (hopefully) no fluff, and (definitely) no BS guide to what security culture is, how to measure it, and how to shape and strengthen it within your organization.

Why All the Buzz?

For decades, security programs focused on diligently deploying technology-based defenses aimed at keeping cybercriminals at bay. The industry focused on firewalls, intrusion detection and prevention systems (IDSs/IPSs), endpoint protection platforms (EPPs), secure email gateways (SEGs), and more. In truth, the technology has gotten very good. Despite all the focus and spend on security tools, however, the data breach problem is not going away. In fact, it's accelerating faster than the industry can effectively manage via traditional approaches. Figure 1.1 analyzes the amount of money spent on security products since 2007 versus the number of data breaches that occurred each year. The conclusion is clear: The current industry approach is not working.

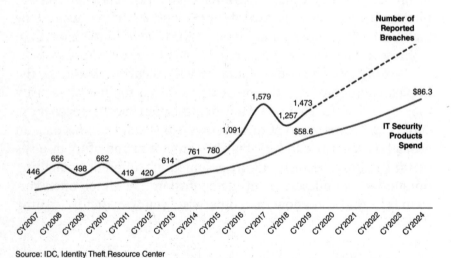

Source: IDC, Identity Theft Resource Center

Figure 1.1   Organizations globally have invested massively on cybersecurity, yet breaches continue to increase.

And here's where the buzz about security culture comes in. Leaders are realizing two things:

- Technology-based defenses have gotten so good that attackers are being pushed to hack humans rather than spending weeks, months, or years researching and developing effective attacks to defeat technology-based defenses.
- Humans are now the primary attack vector. As such, it's imperative to strengthen the human layer of security.

These two realizations (illustrated in Figure 1.2) have led to a growing interest in human layer defense. This isn't to replace any of the technology-based layers—those are still needed. But this is to strengthen a much-needed additional defensive layer.

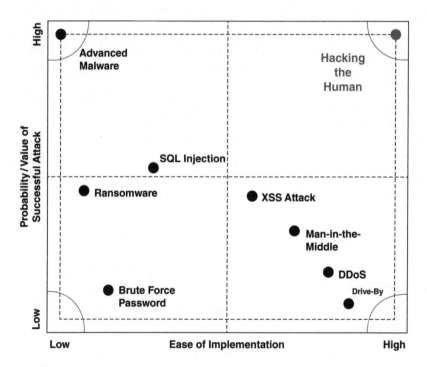

Figure 1.2 Hacking the human yields the highest ROI for attackers.

If you need more evidence that traditional technology-centric approaches to security are ineffective at stemming the tide of data

The Technology-Based Defense vs. Human-Based Defense Debate: A False Dilemma

You've undoubtedly been presented with this dilemma before. Someone says that it's worthless to focus on the human side of security because, no matter what, there will always be someone who will fall for a phishing email or make some other error. In short, their argument is that the human defense isn't 100 percent effective, so it can't be relied on and doesn't deserve an investment of time, energy, or funding.

You'll even hear some make claims to the effect of, "only technology will help an organization prevent security issues." This type of thinking has been prevalent in security circles for decades and has led to the situation that we're in right now, where the human layer has been neglected.

A quote from the preface of Bruce Schneier's book *Secrets and Lies* is fitting here. Bruce ends the preface with these words, "[a] few years ago I heard a quotation, and I am going to modify it here: If you think technology can solve your security problems, then you don't understand the problems and you don't understand the technology" (Schneier, 2000).

The following is an excerpt from Perry's book, *Transformational Security Awareness: What Neuroscientists, Storytellers, and Marketers Can Teach Us About Driving Secure Behaviors* (Carpenter, 2019). The excerpt does a good job summarizing why this is a false dichotomy. This shouldn't be presented as an either/or dilemma.

> As an industry, we will always have to solve (and evolve) for both sides of the equation (technology and humanity). Not implementing standard and reasonable technology-based tools proven to improve an organization's security posture would be negligent. Similarly, not acknowledging

that technology will never be 100 percent effective at preventing cybercriminals from creating well-crafted attacks targeting humans, such as emails or other messages that reach your end users, is also negligent. Neither approach is mutually exclusive of the other. And whenever we create stronger security protocols intended to help our organizations, there will be a group of employees who will intentionally or unintentionally find ways to bypass those controls. The human element must be a factor in the deployment of technology, and it should be understood as a security layer in and of itself. Your defense-in-depth security strategy should always account for the following:

- Determined human attackers who are continually probing for flaws within your security technologies (and that flaws will always exist)
- Unwitting employees who find themselves on the receiving end of a cybercriminal seeking to accomplish their goals by going around the technical layers of an organization's defenses, targeting humans instead
- Employees who negligently or intentionally circumvent technical controls
- Employees who negligently or intentionally divert from the organization's policies, controls, and processes
- The interdependency between policies, controls, and processes that exist in the physical world and those of the organization's technology-based systems
- The ever-evolving ecosystem of mobile, IoT, and other new technology-based systems that your people will engage with
- The reality that digital data can easily spill into the physical world (e.g., printouts, whiteboards, conversations, and so on)

Thinking about this, we can safely conclude that the human element of security will always be something that deserves intentional focus.

breaches, then you owe it to yourself to have a look at Verizon's Data Breach Investigation Report (DBIR). Each year, the Verizon DBIR provides a deep analysis into the types and causes of data breaches. And each year, they find that a vast majority of data breaches are caused by some form of exploitation of the human element or by human error. For instance, the most recent report as of this writing, Verizon's 2021 Data Breach Investigation Report, found that of the over 5,250 breaches they analyzed, 85 percent involved the human element (Verizon, 2021; Sheridan, 2021).

It's time to remove our rose-colored techno-centric glasses. Technology cannot and will never block all threats that involve humans. And that's why a focus on security culture is critical.

It's time to remove our rose-colored techno-centric glasses. Technology cannot and will never block all threats that involve humans. And that's why a focus on security culture is critical. This is a rallying call to build up our human layer of defense.

Let's face it. We already know what we have to lose by not focusing on the human layer. Breaches are on the rise. Phishing is on the rise. Ransomware is more rampant and destructive than ever (Register, 2021), growing at a rate of over 150 percent in just the first half of 2021 (Seals, 2021). Cybercriminals are constantly searching for the least fortified aspects of your defenses. It's clear that technology alone will never adequately defend your organization. It's time to move beyond paying lip service to the human side of security. It's time to intentionally focus on building a healthy security culture.

What Is Security Culture, Anyway?

Let's start off with what should be a simple question: What does the phrase *security culture* mean to you? In other words, if you were asked to define security culture, how would you answer?

In November 2019, KnowBe4 commissioned Forrester Consulting to evaluate security culture across global enterprises. The results were eye-opening. Forrester Consulting conducted an online survey with 1,161 respondents who all had managerial duties or higher in security and risk management. The study found that 94 percent of respondents said that security culture is important for business success (KnowBe4, 2020).

Let's face it, Ninety-four percent is big, and getting 94 percent of people to agree on anything can feel like a miracle in today's world. So, these leaders obviously place value on having a strong security culture. But here's the thing: There was no agreement as to what a security culture actually is.

A Problem of Definition

In that study with 1,161 respondents, there were 758 unique definitions given for security culture. Forrester analyzed these 758 unique definitions and broke them into five different categories based on the general sentiment reflected in each of the proposed definitions. Here's the breakdown:

- 29 percent of respondents believed that security culture is compliance with security policies.
- 24 percent said that it was having an awareness and an understanding of security issues.
- 22 percent said that it was a recognition that security is a shared responsibility across the organization.
- 14 percent indicated that it had something to do with establishing formal groups of people that could help influence security decisions.
- 12 percent said that a good security culture meant that security was embedded into the organization.

That's a wide variety of ideas for what security culture is. And it shows the danger of not having a formal, industry-recognized understanding of what this concept really means. Just imagine being in a room where someone is talking about how critical it is to have a good security culture. Now, imagine looking all around the room and seeing virtually everyone (94 percent of the folks in the room) nodding in violent agreement. Seems like a real kumbaya moment, right? Nope. In reality, they are all agreeing to different concepts—preexisting assumptions about what they assume the speaker is referring to, but (and here's the danger) everyone believes they share the same definitional idea. Situations like this belong in Monty Python skits, not as part of the unconscious assumptions driving our security and risk management programs.

Situations like this belong in Monty Python skits, not as part of the unconscious assumptions driving our security and risk management programs.

At this point, you're probably asking yourself which of the five categories we most closely align with. For the most part, we believe that the 12 percent of those who indicated that a good security culture means that security is embedded throughout the organization should get the gold star. Respondents in this category made statements like, "we put security in high regard throughout the company."

Your humble authors believe this is the most accurate representation of what a good security culture is. The definitions offered up within the other categories would naturally flow from this. Having security embedded throughout the organization and holding security in high regard will result in people following policies, having awareness of issues, and recognizing that security is a shared responsibility, and the intentional creation of groups who would serve as security advocates and liaisons.

Let's be clear. We believe that 12 percent of people offered a directionally correct response. But the other 88 percent of respondents also offered valuable insights. They offered ideas of things that we might consider evidence (or artifacts) of a good security culture.

We, as an industry, have a lot of work to do in making this idea of "embeddedness" and "high regard" something that is synonymous with how people generally define security culture. This understanding indicates much more than what surface-level security awareness can accomplish. It indicates a much deeper appreciation and value of security than simple policy acknowledgments or compliance will ever offer. This is something else—something different from the status quo.

A Problem of Overconfidence

The Forrester Consulting study also found that security leaders are overconfident that they have a good security culture. That's obviously not a good thing. Overconfidence means they believe that they've got things under control. These leaders have a semblance of security in their mind, and yet they're leaving themselves extremely vulnerable. They are, quite literally, operating under a false sense of security.

There's a phrase that I, Perry, have said for years: "A security culture already lives and breathes in every organization. The question is really, how strong, intentional, and sustainable is that security-related aspect of your organizational culture? And what do you need to do about it?"

A security culture already lives and breathes in every organization. The question is really, how strong, intentional, and sustainable is that security-related aspect of your organizational culture? And what do you need to do about it?

There are already embedded security-related attitudes, beliefs, values, behaviors, and social norms in every organization. Your goal as a leader is to be intentional about how you pinpoint and measure security-related aspects of the culture and how you intentionally shape those aspects. That means you must be proactive about security culture management.

You need to understand how that can become part of your larger organizational culture management initiatives. Ultimately, you want security beliefs, values, behaviors, and social pressures woven all throughout the fabric of your larger organizational culture. The takeaway here is that you already have a security culture. What are you going to do with (or about) it?

You can't treat security culture as a black box topic. Security culture does not exist as an entity unto itself. You already have a security culture, whether you like it or not and whether it is good or not. Security culture is inexorably intertwined within your larger organizational culture. The question you need to deal with is what are you going to do with (or about) these security-related aspects of your larger organizational culture?

It's your move.

Takeaways

- Security and business leaders are realizing that humans are a critical layer within their security programs.
- Recognizing humans as an important layer in your security program does not negate the importance of technical defenses.
- The question isn't whether or not you have a security culture; it's how you need to engage it.
- Leaders agree that security culture is a critical aspect of risk reduction, but there is little agreement on what constitutes a good security culture.
- Security leaders are often overconfident in the maturity of their security culture, resulting in a false sense of security.
- This book will give you the necessary information and tools to begin shaping your security culture.

Chapter 2
Up-leveling the Conversation: Security Culture Is a Board-level Concern

Management is efficiency in climbing the ladder of success; leadership determines whether the ladder is leaning against the right wall.

Stephen Covey

Let's be honest—no organization will ever be fully secure. Security is a management process. It's the process of managing all the risks and threats that arise minute by minute, hour by hour, and day by day. You are never done. You can be more secure than you were yesterday, but you never arrive. You're always a zero-day threat, misconfiguration, or employee-related incident away from being less secure than you were just a minute ago.

This is a critical concept for organizational leaders and their boards of directors. So, if you are one of those leaders, or if you have influence over one of those leaders, read on. This chapter will serve as an overview of why security culture and your human-layer defenses deserve attention at the highest levels of your organization. And, while we don't want to be fear mongers or party killers, we will also briefly discuss the cost of ignoring your security culture or taking it for granted. Lastly, we'll point you to some valuable resources that you can begin using right away.

A View from the Top

If there is one good thing that comes from all the media reporting about cyber breaches around the world, it is that virtually every organization now recognizes the need to shore up their cyber defenses. Along with that recognition comes the need to communicate clearly throughout the executive team and board of directors about the organization's risks and cyber readiness. This isn't to say that every member of the board of directors and executive team needs to become an expert in cybersecurity in addition to their current expertise, but they do need to become experts in understanding the risks that cyber-related events might have on the business.

Risk is the key word. Executives manage based on risk, reward, and opportunity. Conversations about security for the sake of security will have limited value. They might be interesting, but they aren't particularly useful. Useful conversations are those that provide context about how cybersecurity concepts and decisions might impact the business, either positively or negatively.

Here's a way of framing conversations we've found works for making virtually any topic understandable and relatable at an executive level. Think of it as a simple filter or formula you can use to improve your executive communication:

information → story / narrative → transparency and metrics → insight and direction

Information informs your story/narrative, which is then interpreted clearly and honestly via the metrics and anecdotes you use, leading to insights and future direction. We know that formula might feel obvious; you might have even thought something along the lines of, *"Well, duh!"* But now be honest with yourself and remember that you (like most people) very likely tend to try to dazzle with details. And that's the problem. Stories might include details, but details are not stories. Context might include details, but details don't provide context on their own. Any time you provide a data point, you need to clearly state what that means and why that matters in the grand scheme of things. This is where most security executives fail.

If you aren't clearly telling your own story and articulating what your data and details imply, then your audience is left to interpret things for themselves. They form an alternate story in their minds, and that's not usually to your benefit.

If you aren't clearly telling your own story and articulating what your data and details imply, then your audience is left to interpret things for themselves. They form an alternate story in their minds, and that's not usually to your benefit.

They make assumptions, and those assumptions might not align with reality. That's why it's so important to have a clear understanding of the information you need to share and the story that it tells. After you understand your information and broader narrative, you can work on underpinning that story with relevant metrics and anecdotes. And then you can point back to your metrics, anecdotes, and story to bring your audience to the ultimate conclusions. This is your chance to celebrate your successes, set future expectations, gain feedback, solicit support, and more.

Telling the Human Side of the Story

When it comes to cybersecurity, there is a story about securing your organization's future by providing long-term resilience and sustainability. And, yeah, there are certainly aspects of that story that are technology-centric, but there are also many, many aspects that are people-centric. When leaders hyper focus on the technology side of the story, they risk forgetting that technology is only part of the equation. And they risk forgetting that humans are at the center of everything.

Much of the cybersecurity narrative revolves around technology. We talk about firewalls being bypassed, data being leaked, or servers being hacked; we show images of cybercriminals in dark rooms surrounded by screens filled with indecipherable computer code. When that's the picture of cybersecurity that our people get, it is very easy for them to feel overwhelmed. Making human-layer vulnerabilities and defenses a frequent and explicit part of your organization's cybersecurity conversations paves the way for more human-centric policies, processes, and technologies.

By consistently referring to the importance of the human layer, you can reinforce the need to engage people. It gives everyone the message that your people share a proactive role helping protect the organization. It opens up more meaningful conversations and helps pave the way to gain buy-in for initiatives that will help foster a stronger security culture.

What's the Cost of Not Getting This Right?

Organizations can't afford to neglect the importance of the human side of cybersecurity. As we mentioned in Chapter 1, organizations have been investing more and more each year trying to combat cybercrime and data breaches, and yet the breaches keep on coming. In fact, as we showed in Figure 1.1, the rise in breaches is outpacing the global spend on cybersecurity "solutions." Why is that spend not paying off? The reason becomes clear when you look at where the security spend is going.

Figure 2.1 illustrates the problem well. We know that 85 percent of data breaches are being caused by social engineering or human error (Verizon, 2021). But, when you look at organizational spending on security, it becomes clear that leaders have been placing their faith (as reflected by spend) in the wrong areas. Organizations have been focusing on an outdated perimeter-based model of security—one that virtually ignores the human element or hopes that technology-based defenses will suddenly become effective at addressing social engineering and human error in a meaningful way.

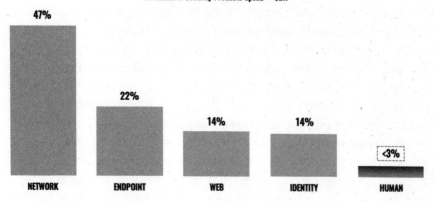

Security Spending Reflects an Outdated/Ineffective Mindset

Worldwide IT Security Products Spend - $BN

Figure 2.1 Cybersecurity spending has effectively ignored the main cause of data breaches

---

Does the Breach Problem Mean Security Awareness Has Failed?

At this point, you might be thinking something like, "But I bet most of those organizations that were breached weren't totally ignoring the human side of things. Surely they were doing some form of awareness training. So what gives? Doesn't that mean that focusing on humans hasn't been effective?"

That's a great question.

The answer isn't that focusing on humans has been ineffective; what's ineffective are the *traditional methods* of

(continued)

(continued)

security awareness and training. Traditional awareness programs focused on sending people information about current threats, security best practices, and policy expectations, and then simply expecting people to magically do the right thing. Every parent or teacher knows that simply exposing people to information and expectations doesn't change behavior, but somehow the security industry duped itself into believing that it would work for us. Obviously it hasn't.

The entirety of this book is about taking *real* control of your human-layer defenses. This will require you to expand your thinking about what security awareness training should look like.

We'll begin that journey in Chapter 3, "The Foundations of Transformation"!

Let's think about this for a minute. Less than 3 percent of security spending is focused on the human layer, but more than 85 percent of breaches are traced back to humans. That stark contrast between the problem area and where organizations are focusing is shocking.

Less than 3 percent of security spending is focused on the human layer, but more than 85 percent of breaches are traced back to humans.

For decades, security leaders have known that humans are the most enticing and vulnerable attack surface; nonetheless, we, as an industry, have tried everything but doing the actual work needed to improve our situation.

And here we are.

Cybercriminals Are Doubling Down on Their Attacks Against Your Employees

Over the past few years, we've seen a meteoric rise in attacks seeking to bypass technology by targeting humans. And it's working. Ransomware continues to make headlines due to large-scale attacks like those that targeted Colonial Pipeline (Fung, 2021), JBS Foods (Reuters, 2021), and Kaseya (Hill, 2021). The recent global pandemic only added fuel to the fire. All of a sudden, organizations and employees were having to adapt to a new normal: working from home. Organizations scrambled to find ways to allow employees to work remotely and safely.

The added confusion and chaos of a global pandemic, employees facing new routines and dealing with new systems, and people feeling more stressed and less connected than ever have all come together to create an enticing playground for social engineers.

The added confusion and chaos of a global pandemic, employees facing new routines and dealing with new systems, and people feeling more stressed and less connected than ever have all come together to create an enticing playground for social engineers. And they are taking advantage of it.

How Bad Is the Problem of Ransomware?

Cybersecurity Ventures recently published its forecast for the growth of ransomware over the next 10 years. It's not good. By 2031, "[r]ansomware is expected to attack a business, consumer, or device every 2 seconds [...] up from every 11 seconds in 2021" (Braue, 2021).

Here are a just a few points to help put the problem into perspective (as of 2021):

- Over one-third of organizations globally have been hit by ransomware (International Data Corporation, 2021).
- Of those hit, roughly 87 percent ended up paying the ransom (International Data Corporation, 2021).
- We are now at a point where ransomware isn't just about making your data inaccessible; it's about exfiltrating the data, using it for extortion against multiple parties, and generally doing everything possible to gain leverage and destabilize your organization. You have no choice but to assume that a ransomware incident is a data breach (Sjouwerman, 2021).
- Social engineering via phishing, vishing (voice phishing), smishing (phishing via text message), and social media are all on the rise (Phishlabs, 2021; Martens, 2021).
- The global average cost of a data breach is $4.24 million (IBM, 2021).
- The global average cost of a ransomware attack is $4.62 million (IBM, 2021).
- The average per-record cost of a data breach is $161. That goes up to $180 if the record contains customer personally identifiable information (PII) (IBM, 2021).

All of this rises to the level of materiality. And material risk is one of the most important things that an executive team and board of directors is concerned with. This is why it is so important to make your human layer of defense a central part of your cybersecurity narrative.

Your People and Security Culture Are at the Center of Everything

Your people are the most important element of your cybersecurity program; ignore them at your peril. Technology will only get you so far. So it's time to elevate human-layer defense to the forefront of the conversation. And it's time to deliberately and methodically focus on security culture.

Human knowledge, beliefs, values, behaviors, expectations, and social pressures are involved in everything that matters within your organization:

- Humans decide what technologies to purchase.
- Humans decide what risks to focus on and how to gain visibility into those risks.
- Humans determine the need for new processes.
- Humans review and tweak the settings of business technologies.
- Humans are in charge of running, patching, and maintaining your security technologies.
- Humans design and code the applications you develop in-house.
- Humans review your third-party risk.
- Humans decide how they will respond to something that looks suspicious.
- Humans decide (both consciously and unconsciously) how they will react to the systems and information they interact with each day.
- Everyone you hire, contract, interact with, or sell to is human.
- Everything you design, sell, or develop business from is ultimately in service of humans.
- Everything and everyone in your organization is impacted by the decisions, behaviors, and expectations of other humans.

Your people and your security culture are the heart of your cybersecurity program. In this book, we'll share a number of interesting (and maybe even shocking) insights related to how your security culture will either be a net benefit or a huge liability for your organization. Here's an example.

While evaluating our security culture dataset, Kai's team recently made an interesting discovery. They took a sample of just over 1,100 organizations and nearly 100,000 employees and looked at employee susceptibility to phishing (measured via a simulated phishing test) as it relates to an organization's overall security culture (as measured by our Security Culture Survey) (Eriksen, 2021). There was one obvious correlation, which you are probably already anticipating: Organizations with a "poor" security culture had more employees who opened and interacted with phishing emails in various ways than employees in organizations with a "good" security culture. Yeah, we would expect that. But here's what we didn't expect: Employees of organizations rated as having a "poor" security culture were 52 times more likely to enter credentials as part of a phishing scam than organizations with a "good" security culture.

Let's put that into raw numbers. In organizations with a "good" security culture, one employee out of 1,000 is likely to be tricked into giving away their credentials or entering other sensitive data as part of a phishing scam. But, in organizations with a "poor" security culture, that number jumps to 1 out of 20.

Our data shows that, in organizations with a "poor" security culture, 1 employee out of 20 is likely to be tricked into giving away credentials or entering other sensitive data as part of a phishing scam. That's in stark contrast to organizations with a "good" security culture, where that number is reduced to 1 out of 1,000.

That's just one stat and one way of measuring the benefit of having a good security culture, but it makes the point: Focusing on your security culture is critical to your overall cybersecurity program and critical to the overall risk posture of your organization.

The Implication

Executive teams and boards of directors need to view security culture as a critical priority. While cybersecurity is a top-of-mind issue for many companies, it can be difficult to ensure that the right information is being shared at the top levels of the organization. To an extent, that's understandable; cybersecurity can seem like an abstract concept. It requires technical knowledge and expertise that can be difficult to translate into business-speak. And, when you don't know how to ask about or measure something, it's easy to ignore it altogether.

Traditionally, the board of directors required reporting based on an increasing risk to the business. For example, back in the early 2000s, the threat of computer viruses wasn't on the radar at the board level; it rarely rose higher than senior IT leadership. However, as the impact of data breaches, destruction of complete networks, and direct monetary theft became a reality, corporate boards took notice. They ramped up the reporting requirements, wanting increased visibility into their defenses. They even created new roles, such as CISO, that often had direct reporting to the CEO or even the board.

Ransomware, social engineering, and human error have proven to be an existential threat to businesses of all sizes.

> *Ransomware, social engineering, and human error have proven to be an existential threat to businesses of all sizes.*

Intellectual property theft, multi-step extortion, customer and employee data theft, multimillion dollar ransom payoffs, brand and reputation damage via released emails, and other public shaming are all taking a toll; and boards of directors are looking for visibility into how vulnerable their organization is and what needs to be done to decrease risk and increase resilience.

Organizations must address ransomware as one of the primary overall risks to the business that must be mitigated, similar to natural disasters. The most common (and easiest path) for ransomware infection is through social engineering attacks on an organization's employees. So, social engineering, which is mitigated only by a mature security culture, deserves board-level attention.

Boards of directors need transparency and accuracy (Internet Security Alliance, 2020). To that end, we'll show you how to accurately measure your security culture. Further, we'll give you the information and tools you need to actively begin strengthening the weak areas and fostering sustainability in the areas where your people are already doing well.

Measuring security culture with the tools and methods we'll show you provides the board a very objective measurement for the company's proactive security measures for the company's largest vulnerability: attacks that succeed by exploiting your human layer.

Getting It Right

We know that traditional technology-centric approaches to cybersecurity haven't proven effective, and the traditional information-centric approach to security awareness hasn't adequately prepared employees for the onslaught of social engineering attacks targeting them. If 85 percent of breaches are being caused by social engineering or human error, and less than 3 percent of spending is focused on the human layer, then it is clearly time to put more focus on the human side.

Information-centric security awareness isn't sufficient. We need a broader approach. We need to focus on the ABCs of cybersecurity: awareness, behavior, and culture. In Chapter 3, we'll discuss key reasons why traditional security awareness programs have fallen short and show how you can transform your program, making it truly effective. You'll learn how principles from marketing, behavior science, and organizational culture management can all be used to drive secure behaviors and foster a workforce that values security.

Takeaways

- Human-layer defenses and your organization's security culture should be key conversation topics within the executive team and board of directors.
- If you aren't clearly telling your own story and articulating what your data and details imply, then your audience is left to interpret things for themselves.
- Ransomware, social engineering, and human error have proven to be an existential threat to businesses of all sizes.
- Less than 3 percent of security spending is focused on the human layer, but over 85 percent of breaches are traced back to humans. It's time to invest more time, money, and effort in the human layer.
- Human knowledge, beliefs, values, behaviors, expectations, and social pressures are involved in everything that matters within your organization.

Chapter 3
The Foundations
of Transformation

Nothing happens until the pain of remaining the same outweighs
the pain of change.

Arthur Burt

We've discussed why security culture is becoming a hot topic and
why it is so important that it deserves board-level attention. But
what about *awareness*? And what about all the other things generally associated with awareness, like simulated phishing tests?
Where do they fit in?

Those are great questions.

The answer is both simple and complex. Those things are
important to culture, but they are not culture. They are pieces of the
puzzle, but they are not the entire puzzle. They are both *artifacts of*
culture, and *instruments* that can be used to *influence* culture. Culture exists anywhere there are people. And a *security* culture exists
anywhere there are people. You have a security culture even if you
aren't focusing on it. The question comes down to whether your

security culture is one that reflects the knowledge, values, norms, and behaviors you want—and what you need to do about it.

> We define "security culture" as being the ideas, customs, and social behaviors of a group that influence its security.

Back in 2019, I (Perry) wrote a book titled, *Transformational Security Awareness: What Neuroscientists, Storytellers, and Marketers Can Teach Us About Driving Secure Behaviors* (Wiley). The book was rattling around in my head for 10 years or so. It was the book I hoped to find when I started out as an awareness practitioner. Since its publication, *Transformational Security Awareness* has gone on to become a standard reference within the security awareness community and was even inducted into the Cybersecurity Canon Hall of Fame (Institute for Cybersecurity & Digital Trust, 2022).

Since its publishing, Transformational Security Awareness *has gone on to become a standard reference within the security awareness community and was even inducted into the Cybersecurity Canon Hall of Fame.*

If you are looking for a book that really gets into the nuts and bolts of running a security awareness campaign, choosing content, developing behavioral interventions, and having a culture mindset, then you'll want to add that book to your reading list.

This book—the book you are reading right now—narrows in on the topic of security culture. It's about tackling the topic of security culture with laser focus and in much more depth than currently available in other books. But, because any serious discussion of security culture cannot exist within a vacuum, I believe there are a few foundational concepts I need to bring forward from *Transformational Security Awareness*. I'll also use this chapter as an opportunity to extend a few of these concepts and help set the stage for areas that we'll cover later in the book.

The Core Thesis

The ideas in *Transformational Security Awareness* revolve around a central thesis: that we cannot afford to ignore the human side of the cybersecurity equation; that technology alone will never be enough to create secure scenarios; and that everything we do or create needs to account for human nature.

"Security awareness" has gotten a bad rap not because it is ineffective but because many organizations running security awareness programs mistakenly believed that simply telling employees what's expected of them or simply alerting employees to threats will lead to a more secure environment.

Let's face it, giving people information doesn't guarantee that they will do any of the following:

- Understand the information
- Remember the information
- Ascribe value to the information
- Apply the information
- Act on the information

Giving people information is just that. We've transferred the information but have little control over what happens to the information after that. This understanding is encapsulated in what I refer to as the *knowledge-intention-behavior gap*.

The Knowledge-Intention-Behavior Gap

Here's a fundamental truth: We all struggle with behaviors. Sometimes our bodies run on autopilot, not consulting the logical/reasoning part of our minds. That can sometimes help us (like when we instinctively swerve our car to avoid an accident), and at other times, that type of automatic behavior can hurt us. Here's an example that I gave in *Transformational Security Awareness*:

> Think about times when an object—let's say a pen—has started to roll off your desk, and your arm seemed to quickly reach over and try to catch the pen before it falls to the floor, maybe even knocking over your coffee mug along the way and causing a bigger mess than if you did nothing. What happened? Many times, you didn't consciously decide to try to catch the pen. Your mind quickly processed the situation and made the decision to intervene without consulting your logical self.
>
> *Transformational Security Awareness: What Neuroscientists, Storytellers, and Marketers Can Teach Us About Driving Secure Behaviors, by Perry Carpenter*

In such situations, we are dealing with what I call the *knowledge-intention-behavior gap*. This gap exists because there are so many things that compete for our attention at the point of behavior. We have a whole set of prewritten shortcuts that our minds like to take, and we often make quick, in-the-moment trade-offs that prioritize our short-term comfort over our long-term good. All of this means that we often act in ways that work completely against any knowledge and/or intentions we have.

If you don't believe that's true, just think about the last time you tried to keep a set of New Year's resolutions. You had things that you knew were important, and you fully intended to act differently based on that knowledge. Alas, it's extremely likely that the behavior didn't follow. That very relatable situation is what it is to be human. That is the knowledge-intention-behavior gap in action.

When it comes to the human side of security, we must treat the knowledge-intention-behavior gap as a fundamental law of reality. We need to stop expecting to make people more secure by simply exposing them to more information. Yes, information still has a place, but information isn't our end goal. The ultimate end goal is to influence value systems and behaviors.

Three Realities of Security Awareness

Out of the knowledge-intention-behavior gap flow three realities of security awareness:

1. Just because I'm *aware* doesn't mean that I *care*.
2. If you try to work *against* human nature, you will *fail*.
3. What your employees *do* is much more important than what they *know*.

It can be tempting to simply read these three statements and move on. That would be a mistake. I believe that virtually every security program failing related to the human side of things comes back to one or more of these statements. If your program sends out a lot of great information but your people don't change their behavior, it's because you haven't given them a reason to care. The information was quickly forgotten, or the action/behavior that the information was intended to encourage wasn't designed for it. If your people aren't following your security policies or using the proper tools or procedures to perform certain actions, then it is likely that your policies, processes, or tools are somehow conflicting with human nature. And, I'll say this as clearly as possible: No amount of knowledge has ever prevented a data breach; it is only what someone does at the point of decision (with or without specific knowledge) that will prevent a breach or allow a breach to happen.

No amount of knowledge has ever prevented a data breach; it is only what someone does at the point of decision (with or without specific knowledge) that will prevent a breach or allow a breach to happen.

Program Focus

The implications of these three realities of security awareness point toward the need to focus on behavioral and cultural patterns rather than being satisfied with information-based training. Figure 3.1 first appeared in *Transformational Security Awareness*. It depicts four types of program focus and the benefit associated with each.

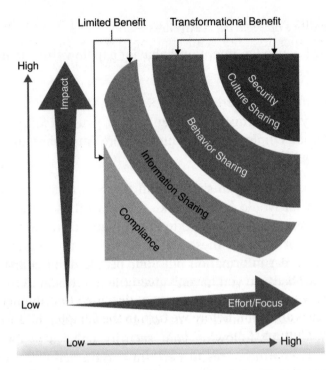

Figure 3.1   Your program's focus will either produce limited benefit or be transformational for your organization.

As you can see, the first type is *compliance*; that's a "check-the-box" approach that produces very little benefit for an organization other than satisfying a regulatory mandate. The next focus type is *information sharing*. This is generally done by well-meaning organizations that believe that sharing information will provide a meaningful result; however, that type of focus will also produce only limited benefit.

The next two program focus types are *behavior shaping* and *security culture shaping*. Each of these require more intentional focus and energy but have the potential of providing a truly transformational benefit to the organization. As you move across the program focus types shown, it's important to note that each of the program types to the right will naturally include all the benefits of the previous types. For instance, information-sharing programs include all the elements required for compliance but also focus on broadening communication. Behavior-shaping programs have done what needs to be done to achieve compliance: add robust communication elements where those can be beneficial, and focus on using behavior design techniques to address human risk. And a *security culture shaping* focus encompasses all those elements *and* leverage techniques to measure and influence the knowledge, beliefs, values, behaviors, and social norms of the employees within an organization.

Extending the Discussion

Okay, now that you have digested the core thesis of *Transformational Security Awareness*, we are ready to spend the rest of this book narrowing in on what a program designed to influence security culture is all about. Before we turn to the Chapter 4, "Just What is Security Culture, Anyway?", however, I first want to introduce an evolution of what was presented in Figure 3.1.

Over the past several months, Kai, myself, and the KnowBe4 Research team have been working on an evidence-backed, data-driven model for accurately measuring the maturity of an organization's security culture. We'll cover this in greater detail in Chapter 12, but it makes sense to introduce you to the model now so that you can see how the material in the forthcoming chapters fits in.

Introducing the Security Culture Maturity Model

As with many maturity models, the Security Culture Maturity Model (SCMM) is loosely based on a Capability Maturity Model (CMM) framework (CMMI Institute Resource Center, 2019). Our model is unique in that it is highly data-driven, based on the insights gathered from over 40,000 global organizations (and growing). As with the CMM, the SCMM has multiple levels, ranging from a level representing very low maturity and progressing up to the pinnacle of achievement. Figure 3.2 depicts the basic structure that most maturity models follow.

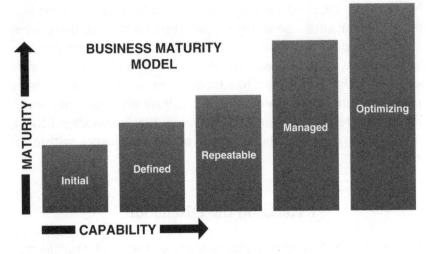

Figure 3.2 Example visualization of a standard/generic maturity model

Figure 3.3 represents another way such models are often represented.

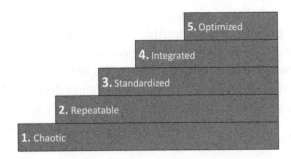

Figure 3.3 Another common maturity model visualization

Each of these representations are good at communicating the building blocks of maturity. They are good at showing the high-level concept, but they lack some of the specific granularity that is useful for business and security leaders. As such, for the purpose of representing maturity within the context of security culture, we created the model represented in Figure 3.4.

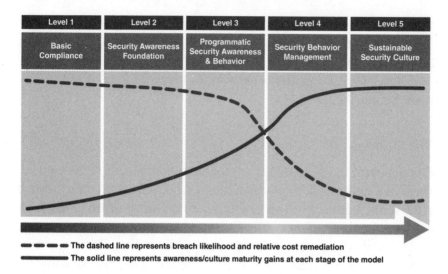

Level 1	Level 2	Level 3	Level 4	Level 5
Basic Compliance	Security Awareness Foundation	Programmatic Security Awareness & Behavior	Security Behavior Management	Sustainable Security Culture

▬ ▬ ▬ ▬ The dashed line represents breach likelihood and relative cost remediation
▬▬▬▬▬▬▶ The solid line represents awareness/culture maturity gains at each stage of the model

Figure 3.4 The Security Culture Maturity Model

The Security Culture Maturity Model in Brief

The SCMM is an evidence-driven framework for understanding and benchmarking the current security-related maturity of an organization, industry vertical, region, or any measurable group. It comprises five levels. The model's range accounts for organizations with no formal or intentional awareness, behavior, or culture plan other than to achieve basic compliance (level 1), all the way up to the most sophisticated organizations that seek to push beyond the pack and are actively working to shape even the unwritten rules and social dynamics of how their employees value security.

An organization's level of maturity within the SCMM is determined by analyzing all available information regarding an organization's security culture. We call each data point a Culture Maturity Indicator (CMI). We'll take a deeper look at CMIs a bit later in the Chapters 4 and 12. It is important to note that, although much of this analysis can be done automatically using the tools and datasets that Kai and I are developing at KnowBe4 Research, the value of this model is not restricted to KnowBe4 customers. Our intent was to create a model that is vendor agnostic, so we'll be providing suggestions and methods for calculating maturity that can be adopted by non-KnowBe4 customers. We'll make these resources available on the companion website for this book: https://SecurityCultureBook.com.

The S-Curves

One aspect of the SCMM that immediately stands out are the two distinctive S-curves, each of which tells a story. The solid blue S-curve represents the specific awareness, behavior, and culture benefits an organization will achieve at each stage. Notice the inflection points and crossover point for each of the S-curves. The inflection points and crossover point each represent the real behavioral gains that an organization can expect as it begins to focus on shaping employee behavior through a combination of training, frequent simulations, and reinforcement tactics.

Also notice the relationship between the two curves. As security awareness, behavior, and culture increase, the likelihood of human-related breach and cost of remediation (the dotted red S-curve) decrease. Again, there is a sharp inflection point as organizations move beyond knowledge-based awareness and begin intentionally focusing on behavior and the social aspects of how employees value security.

Lastly, there is an additional point reflected in the placement of the curves. There is a gap between the top of the blue line and the top right of the chart, and there is an even more noticeable gap between the very end point of the dotted red line and the bottom point of the final level. These represent a simple truth: No organization will fully "arrive," and no organization will ever fully be beyond the possibility of experiencing a human-related breach. That's the nature of any security measure, technology-based or human-based. No security layer (technical or human) can make an organization 100 percent secure, but each additional layer of security you add provides additional resilience.

To keep from getting too far in the weeds right now, we'll save the detailed discussion of the maturity levels, CMIs, and the application of data to the model for Chapter 12. For now, you can probably see the parallels between this data-driven model (Figure 3.4) and the conceptual model from *Transformational Security Awareness* (Figure 3.1).

The Value of the Security Culture Maturity Model

The SCMM has some interesting properties in that it can communicate at multiple levels. For instance, there is value in being able to quickly communicate what level an organization or vertical is in. There is also value in comparison, where organizations can benchmark themselves against their industry, organizations of comparable size, region, etc.

As you'll see in Chapter 12, the SCMM can be used to communicate at a glance or in extreme detail backed up by rich data. Organizational leaders can visualize their journey and plan the steps required to progress from one level to another. The names of each level are guideposts pointing toward the types of activities that will help the organization progress.

You Are Always Either Building Strength or Allowing Atrophy

Your security awareness, behavior, and culture journey is all about building strength, motor memory, and a sustainable ecosystem. The physical equivalent to this is going to the gym. You don't get in shape by only exercising once. And, if you only exercise once per year, or even once per quarter, you aren't going to see results. The way to create long-term change is to make exercise a part of your lifestyle. This is what traditional security awareness programs get wrong and what organizations that have a check-the-box approach to training get wrong. They implement programs that are the equivalent of going to the gym only once per year.

Lasting change requires lasting commitment. If you stop, you don't stand still—you lose ground.

> *Lasting change requires lasting commitment. If you stop, you don't stand still—you lose ground.*

In the same way that if you stop exercising, your muscles begin to atrophy, your people's awareness, security-related behavior patterns, and security culture maturity will regress if you stop putting in the effort. That's the physics of the situation; as with all things, the law of entropy holds.

Takeaways

- The components of your security awareness program are both *artifacts of* your security culture and *instruments* that can be used to *influence* your culture.
- When it comes to the human side of security, we must treat the *knowledge-intention-behavior gap* as a fundamental law of reality.
- There are three realities of security awareness. 1) Just because I'm *aware* doesn't mean that I *care*. 2) If you try to work *against* human nature, you will *fail*. 3) What your employees *do* is more important than what they *know*.
- Your approach to security culture must be comprehensive and human-centric.
- Security culture can be measured, influenced, and improved.
- We developed the Security Culture Maturity Model (SCMM) as an evidence-driven framework for understanding and benchmarking the current security-related maturity of an organization, industry vertical, region, or any measurable group.
- At all times you are either building strength or allowing atrophy.

Part II

Exploration

Now that we've set the context, let's tease out some of the critical nuances of security culture. In Part II, we further discuss some of the definitional difficulties, bring in some concepts from the social sciences, and then show how security culture comprises a number of different interconnected elements. We cap off this exploration section by hearing from several experts who specialize in organizational culture management.

Chapter 4: Just What Is Security Culture, Anyway?
Chapter 5: Critical Concepts from the Social Sciences
Chapter 6: The Components of Security Culture
Chapter 7: Interviews with Organizational Culture Experts and Academics

Chapter 4
Just What Is Security Culture, Anyway?

Culture can become a "secret weapon" that makes extraordinary things happen.

Jon Katzenbach

Security culture is the backbone of any security program. Every security function, policy, and technology can be traced back to some originating human decision—a human decision that either created the security function or a human decision that made it obvious that a security control was necessary.

The ways in which the human condition plays out within an environment are rarely the product of any single individual; rather, they are the result of how society and technology evolve, which in turn is the result of cultures overlapping and colliding. The function of security lives in this complex exchange of ideas. In this chapter, we seek to untangle some of this complexity and interconnectedness so that you'll have a better idea of how and where *security* fits within the tapestry of culture.

Lessons from Safety Culture

In the 1800s, the discovery of energy sources like oil revolutionized the speed and cost to produce goods. New production plants were built almost everywhere, which created an increase in demand for raw materials, which resulted in new products and, yes, the need for yet more energy. This constant drive for innovation came with another cost: a human cost that led to deaths and serious injuries for many.

When oil and gas was discovered in the North Sea (a wild and stormy sea between Britain and Norway), a race started. The tumultuous environmental conditions meant that new technologies would need to be developed to help extract this newly found treasure. Developing any new technology is a process of trial and error, often many trials and many errors, each building on the previous in an iterative manner, and finally ending with a product that meets the quality and design needs for the task. During the first decades of the North Sea oil run, many cycles of development were undertaken, each leading to higher production yield and a reduction in the loss of human life.

In the beginning of the North Sea adventure, the industry had little regard toward the workers and their safety. Accidents were a normal part of the working day, and it was generally accepted by the workers, their employers, and the government. As the industry grew, and with it the number and the severity of the accidents, the consensus began to shift: The public demanded a safer working environment. This change in attitude led the government to introduce new regulations and standards, the workers demanded better equipment, and the industry set a new key performance indicator (KPI): the goal of *zero deaths*.

These changes in the oil and gas industry did not happen overnight. It took almost 30 years from the start of the development in the North Sea until regulations and safety became a part of the reality in the late 1970s and early 1980s. From then on, it took close to another 20 years to develop practices and educate the staff—from the board of directors all the way down to those working in the kitchens. At the beginning, the industry claimed it didn't need any regulations. Later, it made the case that it could self-regulate. Interestingly, the changes started to happen only when national and international regulations were put in place by governments, followed by audits, and hefty fines and penalties were levied against those who failed to comply.

This transformation toward a safety culture is not unique for the oil and gas industry. Many, if not all, industries have undergone similar transitions from a maverick mentality into a safety focus. One example is the air traffic industry, where James Reason is a leading force in understanding what constitutes critical building blocks for building and maintaining good cultures. Reason explains that "human error is both universal and inevitable" (Dunn, 2014). In other words, we humans are fallible. We make mistakes. These mistakes are part of our nature and should be expected. Therefore, Reason concludes that, although we may not be able to change the human condition, we can change the conditions in which humans operate.

[A]lthough we may not be able to change the human condition, we can change the conditions in which humans operate.

This insight is crucial: Instead of trying to make people do things that are against human nature, we can—and should—change the nature of the environment we are functioning within. From a safety perspective, this can mean wearing hard-hats, building fences, and using clearly marked signs. In a medical facility, it is the establishment of sterilized zones, clearly marked areas for disposal of biohazardous waste, and the establishment of access-controlled rooms for housing pharmaceuticals. All these measures are put in place to help allow humans to do their jobs as safely as possible within their environments.

What's the Difference Between *Safety* and *Security*?

The difference between *safety* and *security* is simple: *Safety* is about protection in the physical realm (something we as humans can easily relate to), whereas *security* is mainly about protecting something abstract, like information. This difference is important to keep in mind when working with the human element of security. It leads us to ask questions that help bridge the gap between what we know about the physical world and how we can imagine a digital equivalent. Examples include questions like

- What is the virtual equivalent to having people wear a hard-hat on their computer?
- How do you create something like a physical "keep out" fence in computer systems or networks?
- What's the digital equivalent of a sterile zone, hazardous waste removal, or locking up pharmaceuticals?

In other words, how can we make the abstract concepts related to *security* as easily recognizable and actionable as *safety* is considered today?

A Jumble of Terms

Security culture as a concept can be viewed through several different lenses, each providing perspectives that may help in prioritizing what is needed. Using different lenses can be very valuable when focusing on specific areas or details. The drawback, however, is that a specific focus also removes other elements that may be relevant to consider.

When we talk about security culture, we consider the term broadly. It is used to discuss security awareness, behavior, and culture at a high level. This allows us to discuss the topic in general terms, thus providing broad usage. You may also come across more specific terms, like *information security culture, IT security culture,* or *cybersecurity culture.* These are all security culture but with a somewhat narrower focus. This narrowed focus is unlikely to provide any added value to the discussion of security culture from a business perspective. However, we believe it may be helpful to provide a brief understanding of the different terms and their focus as a way of illustrating the shifting lens of security culture.

Information Security Culture

Information security culture points to the area of *information security.* The focus here is on the protection of *information* in any form. As a concept, information security has been around for thousands of years. We know that the Romans invented procedures and methods for protecting information and to ensure the information reached the right destination. Information security is not *limited* by technology; it concerns itself with information in any form and in any place, including information that resides inside the minds of employees. One example of information security is the awareness campaign by the United States during World War II: "Loose lips sink ships." The CIA triad (confidentiality, integrity, and availability) of information security is often considered a core principle of information security (Chai, 2021).

IT Security Culture

IT security culture is a subset of information security culture. It concerns itself mainly with the culture around securing the IT systems of an organization. IT security limits its focus to information (i.e., data) created, stored, transmitted, or manipulated by a computing device or network. Fifty years ago, this was a very small subset of all information available. Today, things are much different. Most information available today is stored or transmitted through some form of computing device. As a result, IT security has become a major part of information security since the 1990s. IT security culture is often technical in nature, focusing on the knowledge and use of computer systems. The term *IT security* is often used interchangeably with *cybersecurity*, but there are some minor differences.

Cybersecurity Culture

Cybersecurity culture is often used interchangeably with IT security culture and sometimes interchangeably with information security culture. Cybersecurity concerns itself with the systems used to create, manipulate, store, and consume information. Unlike IT security, where computers may not be connected to a broader network like the Internet, it is generally accepted that cybersecurity focuses on computers and systems that are connected to the Internet, directly or indirectly. Cybersecurity is also concerned with the entire ecosystem of computing devices, not just the ones that humans interact with directly. That means that the cybersecurity domain also includes IoT, command and control systems, and so on. Cybersecurity can be extremely technical and complex, often protecting cloud computing systems that involve automatic scaling, orchestration, and many levels of abstraction.

It is our belief that in most cases, the reader of this book does not need to be a specialist on these subcultures of security culture. Just be alert for times when someone speaking or writing about security culture may actually intend to refer to a subdomain of security culture rather than something more overarching.

Security Culture in the Modern Day

We argue that security culture has been around since the dawn of time and even that some other species have their own security cultures. As interesting as that is, however, it is more relevant to consider security culture since the dawn of the Internet. Before the Internet, security culture was mostly technology-agnostic, as it mainly focused on the protection of information (information security) or the protection of real-world assets (security/physical security). With the incredible growth of the Internet, security culture had to evolve quickly and dramatically. This evolution of security culture progressed in three steps: *technology focus*, *compliance focus*, and, finally, a focus on dealing with the *human reality* of the issues.

Technology Focus

When the Internet was born in the late 1960s, the main idea and priority was to create a nationwide network within the United States to ensure that critical information could be sent and received by the government in case of a nuclear disaster. The primary focus of the design was the *A* in the CIA triangle: *accessibility*. It was critical that the information reached its destination. *Confidentiality* and *integrity* were of lesser concern due to external security measures; only select personnel with the appropriate security clearance had access to the network.

This may have been reasonable during the Cold War, but it introduced a host of challenges later when the same technology was opened to use for anyone, clearance or no clearance. This backdrop helps us understand why some of the IT security issues we face today are so persistent. It's because the foundation of the Internet—the system that most companies, countries, and people use to communicate in the modern era—is built on top of a technology stack that was not designed to *protect* information. It was built to *deliver* it.

In the 1990s, as the Internet saw its global adoption, it became clear that not everything connected to the Internet should be available to everyone. An organization's server could include internal information that it never intended to be available from the outside, yet often it was easy to find for anyone who cared to look for it. Another challenge was that the technology was built with the idea that *we trust people to use it appropriately*. The implied idea that *no one will intentionally try to sabotage or break things* was a remnant of the early Internet days, and one that meant many servers and systems were open for anyone to use. We just trusted people not to take advantage. One of the first demonstrations of the lack of IT security was the first recorded Internet worm in 1988. The Morris worm provided clear evidence that the technology was not at all secure just because we tend to trust the users on the system.

Throughout the 1990s, technology-based controls were introduced to reduce risk. Firewalls and antivirus software are probably the two most well-known of these technologies. IT specialists, who back then were more IT generalists than anything else, had to learn how to harden systems, how to set up routing tables and firewall rules, and to clean up the mess when something broke. The focus was on technology, and for many of us, it was a great time to be in IT.

Compliance Focus

As businesses and governments moved to computers and connected to the Internet, another perspective of security came into play: legal risk. Legal frameworks did not exist in the beginning, so lawyers had an interesting time trying to understand the boundaries of technology, jurisdiction, and how information flows. Who is responsible for a security leak? What about music and movies that surfaced on servers located in a country outside of your jurisdiction? What about software and other intellectual properties being distributed illegally?

The late 1990s and forward has seen a focus on the legal side of risk management. Regulations from industries and from governmental bodies around the world emerged. Many such regulations require organizations to train their employees on security concepts; however, most of the regulations do not provide guidance related to the finer details around what exactly should be covered and how often those topics should be covered by the training. As such, many employees saw the new, annual, and mandatory security training emerge, a training that often was long, boring, and not relatable to most employees. And, even if some organizations did their best to make the most of the training content, most just focused on the bare minimum to satisfy the legal requirement for complying with the regulation.

Many organizations today still operate under a compliance-focused mindset. The good news is that, because of the extreme number of security incidents over the past decade, most organizations today recognize the need to up their game. They are moving on to addressing the problem by embracing the inherent realities in human nature and culture.

Many organizations today still operate under a compliance-focused mindset. The good news is that, because of the extreme number of security incidents over the past decade, most organizations today recognize the need to up their game. They are moving on to addressing the problem by embracing the inherent realities in human nature and culture.

Human-Reality Focus

Around 2010, some people around the world decided to figure out how to address the realities of how humans interact with technology and with each other. At that time, Kai Roer released his framework for building and maintaining security culture and made it free under a Creative Commons license. In South Africa, Adele Da Veiga, of the University of South Africa School of Computing, decided to explore security culture from an academic perspective and created what is possibly the first academic measurement instrument for security culture. In Norway, Roar Thon, of the Norwegian National Security Authority, advocated security culture as a means to improve national security, which in turn lead to regulatory changes, government mandates, and a national focus on improving security culture. All of this coincides with a similar industry move in the United States. At that time, a few companies in the United States began focusing on evolving the security awareness market by adding more engaging content and by offering real-world security-related behavior shaping via simulated phishing and other simulated social engineering exercises. The addition of direct behavioral interventions within the context of a security awareness program ushered in a new understanding of what security awareness can achieve.

For the next few years, change was slow. But things started to accelerate again in 2015. The criticism of compliance-focused awareness training programs had reached a new high. Regulatory compliance was doing little to stop the surge of a new threat: ransomware. So, organizations around the world (along with regulators) were now actively seeking newer, more human-centric approaches. Terms like *security culture* and *security behavior* started to be used more broadly. And many within the awareness community became much more interested in the science behind human behavior.

Everything revolves around one single element: the human. Ultimately, this reality-focused approach boils down to understanding human nature so well that we can engineer systems, training, processes, policies, and controls (both technical and non-technical) to make it easy to do the right thing and hard to do the wrong thing.

Security Culture Is in the Numbers

Security culture comprises several factors related to knowledge, values, social norms, environment, and more, but one of the great things about security culture is that it is expressed via behaviors. That means that security culture can be measured. A very useful way is to use different sources like employee behaviors as recorded via traditional IT and InfoSec tools. Then, you can couple that real-world behavioral data with the data related to things like training history and content as well as knowledge-based tests and assessments specifically created to measure sentiments and culture. Each single source of information is valuable. Each source represents a collection of Culture Maturity Indicators (CMIs). By combining them, we are able to add precision and clarity to our view of the human side of security.

Takeaways

- Your security culture is the backbone of your security program.
- Lessons about security culture are readily available by looking at parallels in safety culture.
- The evolution of security culture progressed in three steps: *technology focus*, *compliance focus*, and, finally, a focus on dealing with the *human reality* of the issues.
- The large and unending number of data breaches over the past years has primed organizations to move from a *compliance focus* to a *human-reality focus*.
- Security culture is outwardly expressed via security-related behaviors.

Chapter 5
Critical Concepts from the Social Sciences

We think, each of us, that we're much more rational than we are. And we think that we make our decisions because we have good reasons to make them. Even when it's the other way around. We believe in the reasons, because we've already made the decision.

Daniel Kahneman

One of the biggest issues in the field of cybersecurity is that we tend to approach situations with blinders on. We assume that the problems we face are new and unique—and we are often wrong.

We've seen that sense of myopia at play when it comes to security culture as well. There is some good news, however: Security culture isn't as new and mysterious as some believe. Everything related to security culture ultimately comes down to some aspect of human nature, and scientists have been studying human nature for a long time.

In this chapter, we take a brief look at a couple foundational ideas from social science that we believe directly relate to security culture and behavior. This perspective will shed new light on employee behavior, and it will lay the groundwork needed to identify strategies and tactics to apply in your security culture program. It will also help you avoid outdated advice and practices that could otherwise trip you up.

What's the Real Goal—Awareness, Behavior, or Culture?

Over the past several years, our industry has been fixated on the idea that the silver bullet for dealing with the human side of cybersecurity is to find effective ways of managing employee behaviors. After all, if we can implement behavioral methods that will reduce an employee's likelihood of clicking a phishing email, or if we can force people to adopt better behaviors related to password management, then we ultimately shouldn't need to focus on awareness or culture.

To be clear, implementing behavioral controls that result in your employees doing the right thing at the right time is a great goal, but getting there requires a multifaceted approach. Knowledge, social pressures, and the right technologies all have a part to play. An overfocus on any single technology or method is very likely to set you up for failure or leave you with a false sense of security.

An overfocus on any single technology or method is very likely to set you up for failure or leave you with a false sense of security.

Your end goal should be to build an organization where people, process, and technology work together in a fluid and autonomous manner—a virtuous cycle. The end goal is never just one thing, like behavior. It's more complex than that, involving several moving parts that you can use to manage risk at the level required.

Coming to Terms with Our Irrational Nature

It seems that our industry is going through a similar shift in thinking as we have seen in fields of economics and behavioral science: a move away from rational agent theories into behavioral economics, where the agents (people) make decisions based on any number of external and internal influences. These influences include things like emotions, peer pressure, motivation, or any other momentary factor that may come into play at the time of decision-making.

In economics, researchers such as Richard Thaler have worked to debunk the long-held idea that, if someone has all the relevant information available to them, they will surely make the right decision. Along with other scientists such as Amos Tversky and Daniel Kahneman, Thaler has demonstrated again and again that humans base their decisions, and their behaviors, on factors that are not considered within the framework of traditional economic theory. A great introduction to behavioral theory, and the work of Richard Thaler, is found in the book *Misbehaving: The Making of Behavioral Economics* (Thaler, 2015). In this extremely readable book, he looks back through his 40-year tenure as a researcher in behavioral economics and explains every major discovery and discussion he and his fellows have had during his career.

In many ways, Thaler's story echoes our own struggles, as many individuals work to move the field of cybersecurity into the modern world of social sciences. Traditional security awareness training programs have fallen prey to a false assumption; they assume that if an employee simply knows the right thing to do, they will do the right thing. This is a variation of the rational agent theory in economics. And, like the rational agent theory in economics, it is time to put this idea to its final rest.

Let's back up for a second and set some context. In traditional economics and decision theory, humans are referred to as *rational agents*. They are assumed to always perform optimally based on the information they are presented. Factors like emotion and bias aren't part of the equation.

When you think about it, it's not hard to see the weakness in the idea that humans are rational agents. All you have to do is look around the world we live in, consider our own lives and decisions, or remember times when we learned new things. Habits, preferences, biases, and social pressures override rationality—all the time. We humans are not simple computational machines. Because of that, we can't expect people to do the right thing just because they've been exposed to the right information or informed of what is expected of them. A successful security culture management program will take this reality into account.

We Are Lazy

Humans are lazy. We tend to do anything we can to conserve energy. We avoid doing things that we don't have the motivation to do; and even then, we may do something else or look for shortcuts. This can be seen when deciding what to make for dinner after a long workday: At this point, we have exhausted the daily amount of cognitive energy, so making even simple choices can feel overwhelming. Our brain resists putting in the work to decide what to eat. And we don't want to expend the energy required to make a healthy meal, so we choose takeout or use a meal delivery service.

There's an entire app ecosystem that caters (pun intended) to just this situation. But—Oh no—opening the app presents a whole new set of options and choices that can tend to overwhelm. Luckily, the apps we've already used conveniently remember our previous choices, reducing the needed thought and actions to just the tap of an icon to accept the same old pizza from the same old restaurant. Then, finally, we can relax.

Our daily decision-making energy is finite. Unless you are overstressed, exhausted, or in burnout, you generally recover well and are ready for a new day of decision-making when you wake up each morning. In those cases where you are exhausted and overstressed, it seems that even making the simplest decision can be overwhelming and confusing.

From a security standpoint, it's important to be aware that this finite daily pool of mental energy is the same energy used when you decide which emails to open, which links to click, and which forms to complete. It is the same energy that you use to determine if an email is a phishing attack or not. It is the same energy you use to determine if that URL in the text message you just clicked is genuine or not. And guess what: Your brain doesn't want to expend that energy; it wants to revert to laziness. Your brain wants to revert to reflexive, automatic behaviors.

Daniel Kahneman refers to this state of automated, almost free-of-charge decision-making system as *thinking fast*, or System 1 thinking (Kahneman, 2013). System 1 consists of previously learned heuristics (aka shortcuts), or mental models, that are constantly being used by the mind to interpret and filter observational and sensory input, and then react appropriately. Our brain is amazing at making these automatic decisions. Unfortunately, however, there's a downside. Although thinking fast is great at saving time and energy, it is also prone to error. And this more error-prone system of thinking accounts for roughly 95 percent of the decisions we make each day.

Said another way, we are on autopilot about 95 percent of the time. These nearly automatic decisions and behaviors can be fooled into making decisions that are not aligned with your best interests. This is one of the reasons that training is so important. Training helps to correct wrong shortcuts and to create new automatic behaviors.

[W]e are on autopilot about 95 percent of the time.

So, where does cold, calculated logic come into play? That more rational, logical type of decision-making is what Kahneman refers to as *thinking slow*, or System 2. This system produces much more accurate decisional results than System 1, but our minds don't like to be in System 2. The intentional processing and rationalization of information takes effort. So, when we intentionally bring ourselves into a state of System 2 thinking, our minds are constantly trying to get back to the comfort of System 1. Our minds just don't enjoy the process of consciously sifting through all available options, weighing each option against the others, and then coming to a conclusion. The reason for this seems to be written in our DNA. Biologists believe that our brains seek to conserve energy wherever possible because our body may require that mental and caloric energy for things like hunting and gathering food or other basic survival skills. So, it's not just that we have a limited pool of cognitive energy, but we are wired to naturally conserve that resource—and to protect it.

Unfortunately, this biological wiring doesn't serve us well in the information age and beyond.

Unfortunately, this biological wiring doesn't serve us well in the information age and beyond.

Most of us don't need to conserve energy for hunting, gathering, or running from animal predators. Today's equivalent of those activities is primarily online. Compared with our ancestors, most of us spend very little energy moving, and most of our time and energy is spent in front of a computer, making decisions at every keystroke.

This is important to understand. At all times, we can choose to work *with* or *against* human nature. Working against human nature will likely only lead to organizational pain. Instead, prudent security leaders will look for ways to understand and account for human nature as it relates to every aspect of their security and risk management program. The goal is to help channel behavior in ways that will reduce risk. For example, one way you can do this is by aligning processes and policies to the realities of human nature. Account for the business reasons that employees may make certain decisions or exhibit certain actions. If the policy seems difficult for most people to follow, then assume that something within the policy, process, or communication channel is flawed, not the employee.

Another promising area that we hope to see more of is technology that removes options from the employee. A great example of this is modern, cloud-based email services. Due to their scale, these services discover a large percentage of spam and phishing emails very early, and they simply remove these emails automatically. The human must do more work to navigate to a "junk" or "suspicious email" folder to come in contact with those messages. Of course, most people won't exert the effort to do that; they will deal only with what is in front of them.

Another example is a technology that offers just-in-time learning opportunities, provides teachable moments, or creates pattern interrupts to grab the user's attention. Examples of this would include colorful banners that tell the user that an email is potentially dangerous. Of course, even these types of behavioral interventions and attention prompts can run afoul of human nature. Our minds are constantly trying to filter out extraneous input; so, the colorful banner or app notification may work well for a short while, but then you'll need to change things up and find new ways to capture the user's attention.

As technology evolves, we will see more tools emerge that allow organizations to activate real-time behavioral interventions that direct the employee to the right action as they work, similar to a word processor offering to fix your spelling mistakes. This type of individualized, context-aware behavioral feedback will actively find the best ways to work with human nature to help protect the user and reduce organizational risk.

Never Underestimate the Power of Social Pressures

Have you ever noticed how your mannerisms and language patterns subtly change depending on which social group you are in at a given time? We humans are greatly influenced by the behaviors and social norms of those around us. At all times, our minds are seeking comfort and connection.

(continued)

(continued)

Part of that comes through the established bonds that we feel when we are part of a group.

Group dynamics are always pulling toward a norm. Sometimes that norm is clearly stated verbally or in policy, but often there are sets of unwritten rules that are *just the way things are done around here*. Many of our behaviors and values are *caught* rather than *taught*. So, you need to get a firm understanding of your organization's current social norms and group dynamics. You need to understand where these are working for or against you, and then build plans to reinforce what's working and make proactive adjustments where your norms and group dynamics create risk.

Why Don't We Just Give Up?

So, if we humans are lazy, irrational, and flawed, what hope do we have? That's a reasonable question. We may not be rational, but we do have the capacity to continually improve. We continually learn about our weaknesses, and we can find (or learn) ways to mitigate those weaknesses. Understanding how our minds work is central to understanding how to protect ourselves and our organizations. Understanding models, such as System 1 and System 2 thinking, helps us to understand natural employee tendencies, behavioral patterns, and limitations. We can stop being frustrated and instead find productive ways to work with, rather than against, human nature. We can invest in automation, take another look at our processes, consider social pressures, and more. Doing this will help us review and create better policies to ensure that complying with the policy is easy—and, if it's not, then we know that we need to either make the policy easier to follow, find ways of communicating and motivating our people to overcome the behavioral hurdles, or invest in technologies and processes that remove risk and facilitate the secure choice.

Understanding that humans aren't as rational as we might believe makes it easier to appreciate why people like you and me make what might seem like stupid mistakes. It helps us recognize why people might make choices that feel right at the time but are clearly wrong or strange in retrospect. We are all flawed and fickle humans. Our security programs should account for that; they should be human-friendly.

> *We are all flawed and fickle humans. Our security programs should account for that; they should be human-friendly.*

Another point to consider is that human nature has a number of inherent security vulnerabilities baked into it. Fortunately, however, we can create mitigations by taking an eyes-open approach to our inherent weaknesses. We can protect ourselves by developing strategies that protect us from ourselves. The bad guys do this already. They have built an entire criminal industry around exploiting human nature for financial, political, or industrial gain. Our adversaries have a clear understanding of exactly how humans are weak, and they are exploiting it every day. It's up to us to build our defenses and apply countermeasures.

Security Culture—A Part of Organizational Culture

Security culture is often thought of as a separate, distinct concept with a life of its own. The idea is that security culture is something new, something that exists by and for itself, in some special, possibly even secret, location in the organization. But that's not accurate. Security culture is a part of your organizational culture. It is not separate from or even more important than organizational culture. Security culture is a subculture within a larger organizational culture. Just like organizational culture is found throughout the organization, so is it with security culture. Just as organizational culture changes over time, sometimes on purpose, other times because it was not managed properly, the same is true with security culture.

Your security culture needs to be nurtured, it needs direction, and it needs attention. As organizational and security culture expert John R. Childress says, "Culture drifts" and "You get the culture you ignore" (Childress, 2017). To successfully work with organizational culture, you need leadership buy-in. Your organization's executive team should set the direction and take charge through communication, action, and example. The same is true when it comes to security culture, as has been found in more than 34 academic papers over the past decade (Betsy, 2021). Work with your organization's leadership to get their support and use them to front the security culture work to the whole organization—not once, not just at a kick-off or in a video, but continuously. You are always fighting cultural entropy. Culture is continuous work.

Takeaways

- The human mind is wired to be lazy and rely on shortcuts.
- This cognitive wiring doesn't serve us well in the information age and beyond.
- Organizations need to take human nature into account when writing policy, designing processes, or purchasing/deploying technologies.
- Look for opportunities in process- and technology-based controls that offer just-in-time learning opportunities, provide teachable moments, or create pattern interrupts to grab the user's attention.
- You are always fighting cultural entropy. Culture is continuous work.

Chapter 6
The Components of Security Culture

Concerning the challenge we just faced about how to describe things in numbers and definitions, that is the reason for a unity/oneness? For however many things have a plurality of parts and are not merely a complete aggregate but instead some kind of a whole beyond its parts.

Aristotle

The security industry has struggled to define *security culture* for a long time. Security leaders talk about the value of security culture; but, as we've mentioned previously, they tend to do so without precision. This chapter is about adding that needed precision. Specifically, we'll take a deep dive into seven components that together comprise security culture. This is our perspective, developed over many years at the intersection of two worlds: academia and the "in the trenches" practitioners.

Understanding that security culture is composed of these seven components (which we refer to as *dimensions*) is useful. It brings precision and gives us something to observe and measure. We'll also discuss actions that can be taken to manage the security culture of an organization or group by influencing one or more of the components.

A Problem of Definition

Anyone who decides to study security culture will quickly notice something interesting: They discover that nobody seems to agree what this thing we call *security culture* is. There seems to be as many definitions of security culture as there are academic papers on the topic. To make matters worse, very few of the proposed definitions can offer a holistic overview; instead, you are either given fuzzy generalities or are offered a subset of what culture may consist of.

The Academic Perspective

Academic research follows high standards that often require peer review, ethics reviews, and usually focuses on granular detail. This is great when it comes to understanding the nuances and the different impacts that certain behavioral interventions, training messages, or other tactics may have. It is also extremely helpful when examining isolated elements and their relation to other elements of culture. The challenge, though, is that most academic research is very narrowly focused. It only tells a small part of the story, leaving the rest to interpretation or to be tackled in a later study.

Another challenge is that academics from a wide range of scientific fields of study—from computer scientists to psychologists, and from organizational theorists to economists, to name just a few— are looking into security culture from their own perspective without communicating and sharing their learning across the different fields. This means that the growing body of research is fragmented and difficult to follow, and that sometimes the debate feels more like a turf-war than a mutual interest in furthering the field of research.

The upside is that security culture is being researched from all these different angles, which will be extremely helpful to anyone willing to assemble learnings from across all these disciplines.

The final challenge with academic research is the lack of distribution outside of academic circles.

The Practitioner Perspective

Practitioners in our industry agree that security culture is a vital component of their cybersecurity program. As we mentioned in Chapter 1, however, research shows that security practitioners have difficulty agreeing on what security culture is. This may be because the phrase *security culture* is rather new, leading to some confusion. Our industry has talked about *security awareness* for a long time, leading to some security people thinking security culture is just awareness with a new name. Another bias we see, particularly in some industries where safety is key to success, is a definition of security culture as though it is safety culture: dealing with the physical world instead of the abstracted world of information. It is much easier for us as humans to understand how a hard hat will protect our head from falling debris versus understanding how sharing our credentials in a phishing scam can injure us and our employer.

Talk of security culture is sometimes met with skepticism. Is it not only smoke and mirrors? Is it just *awareness* rebranded? This skepticism is warranted. We've seen smoke-and-mirror security culture marketing before. But, thankfully, we've recently seen the market offering a bit more substance. That's encouraging. Some of this might even be due to our own efforts in this space, such as Kai's creation of the Security Culture Framework and the Security Culture Survey (which we'll be covering in the next few chapters), Perry's research and writing around awareness, behavior, and culture, and Kai's research into seven specific dimensions of security culture.

Understanding that security culture is really a combination of several observable and measurable components (or dimensions) is fundamental to finding ways to intentionally influence and improve security culture.

Understanding that security culture is really a combination of several observable and measurable components (or dimensions) is fundamental to finding ways to intentionally influence and improve security culture.

This understanding also allows for clear reporting to executive teams, boards of directors, employees, and more. In fact, these seven dimensions of security culture and the Security Culture Survey form the foundation of another of Kai's efforts: the annual Security Culture Report.

Defining Security Culture

Our current working definition of security culture is as follows:

Security culture is the ideas, customs, and social behaviors of a group that influence its security.

Any culture is the codification of the beliefs, behaviors, and values of a particular people group. So, when you add a security context, you see that a security culture is the codification of everything security-related or security-impacting as it relates to beliefs, behaviors, and values. This perspective is based on a sociological understanding of culture and is useful as a foundation to create a common understanding of what security culture is:

- **Ideas:** Includes values and shared mental patterns, as well as the shared understanding of what is acceptable and not.
- **Customs:** Accounts for the habits and automatic behaviors that are part of the groups' accepted norms, as well as those that are not. They are considered customs because of their automatic and assumed nature.
- **Social behaviors:** Describes the fact that each member of the group is constantly adjusting their behaviors to those acceptable by the group.

This definition may need to be amended in the future, but it gives us everything we need to have a meaningful discussion. However, as Gregor Petrič, PhD, patiently explained in 2015, "This definition is not good enough to allow a scientific measurement instrument to be built. We need a better one." By better, it turned out, he meant a much narrower, more detail-focused definition. That new, narrower, and more detail-focused definition allowed Kai and Gregor to create the first commercially available scientific instrument for measuring security culture.

Security Culture as Dimensions

From a research perspective, we define security culture as a set of seven interdependent dimensions that together capture the phenomenon that we call security culture. Each dimension is found in academic research geared toward the study and measurement of culture from a sociological perspective. As of this writing, our research suggests that these seven dimensions are the most influential cultural elements related to security.[1] Culture is more than just these seven dimensions, and your perspective will often determine which other elements you want to include in your own studies.

Each of the dimensions influences the other dimensions, creating a multitude of layers of influence, both direct and indirect. This complexity is supported by other research in the field—for example, the knowledge-attitude-behavior model proposed by Stephen Allen Robert (Roberts, 2020). This complexity may initially feel overwhelming, but trust us, it pays off. If you want to measure and influence culture, then you need the precision offered by this kind of model.

---

[1] Back when Kai and team first began their formal study of security culture, very little evidence-based research of relevance existed. As of this writing, in 2022, KnowBe4 Research is cooperating with research units around the world to analyze data on millions of employees to refine our theoretical model to match the real world.

The Seven Dimensions of Security Culture

The following are the seven dimensions of security culture. Figure 6.1 represents one way of visualizing how the seven dimensions are interconnected.

1. **Attitudes:** To what extent do employees care about security? Are they positive, neutral, or negative?
2. **Behaviors:** What are considered acceptable behaviors? What do employees see others doing?
3. **Cognition:** What do employees know? How do they learn? How do they apply that knowledge?
4. **Communication:** How is security communicated throughout the organization? To what extent is the leadership involved? Is security considered a core value?
5. **Compliance:** How well do employees adhere to policies and procedures?
6. **Norms:** To what extent are security-related beliefs, behaviors, and values embedded in the norms and unwritten rules of the organization?
7. **Responsibilities:** To what extent do employees feel empowered? To what extent will they help ensure that other employees follow the rules?

Figure 6.1　Visualizing the seven dimensions of security culture

The Seven Dimensions of Security Culture

The seven dimensions of security culture are interdependent. Each one influences the others. This section offers a brief description of what each dimension captures. In Part III of this book, "Transformation," we will explore how you can use these seven dimensions (and other levers) to improve your security culture.

Attitudes

The attitudes employees have toward security is a critical factor. If employees are negative toward security, they are much less likely to abide by the rules and to act securely. For example, research has shown that the best predictor of behaviors is not knowledge (training) but the employee's attitudes toward security. This means that finding ways to foster positive attitudes toward security can be a great strategy to improve behavior.

Behaviors

What employees see other employees do is very impactful on their own behavior. Most people are likely to adopt the behaviors that they see modeled by others when they are in a group. We are also very likely to do what we are told by someone in authority, suggesting that leadership should be actively involved in security.

Cognition

What employees know can influence their behavior. However, just because someone is *aware* doesn't mean that they *care*! And even caring doesn't always translate to behavior. This is what Perry calls the "knowledge-intention-behavior gap." Training is an important part of any security culture program, but it is not the end-all. Instead, consider training as only one of many tools in your toolbox. Support it with strong messaging from the executives and leadership, and make sure the employees understand why security is paramount. Further support your training program through behavior design initiatives and by trying to foster other areas of influence, such as reward and reinforcement systems.

Communication

One of the skills of great leaders is their ability to communicate. Often you will hear them repeat the same vision many times over, in many different forms and forums. Great leaders recognize the importance of setting the agenda and repeating the message so that every employee can understand and relate. Security is no different: If you want it to happen, repeat your values often and find ways to make people talk about it.

Compliance

Organizations need rules to ensure that employees know what is allowed and what is not. Some organizations are very good at implementing policies and incentives, whereas others are not. If your security policies and procedures are not being followed, it may be because employees are unaware of the policies and procedures, or your policies and procedures are too difficult to follow, or because you need other methods and systems to support compliance.

Norms

Norms are the informal rules, those policies of the group that are not written down and formalized. Some norms may contradict policies. People are more likely to follow norms than complying with policies due to perceived peer pressure. Norms in your organization are "just the way things are done around here." Seek out any disconnects between your norms and your policies. Find ways to influence your norms to better align with policy. This is accomplished through a combination of communication, social pressures, behavior design, and traditional training methods.

Responsibilities

An organization where every employee actively takes part in the security program is a good organization. Empowering employees to make relevant security decisions in their workday is a valuable strategy. Likewise, making sure employees understand that even a tiny action can make a huge difference will be important. Try to focus on the positive change the employee can make instead of dreaded and ineffective fearmongering.

The Security Culture Survey

As mentioned previously, one specific application for the seven dimensions is in the Security Culture Survey (KnowBe4, 2022). The Security Culture Survey applies these seven dimensions to measure security culture. Results are reported across each dimension, giving a comprehensive view of the state of an organization's security culture.

A critical goal of measuring culture is to get a picture that is as honest as possible. In other words, we must avoid asking questions that employees will be tempted to answer in ways that they believe will make them look good. Therefore, the Security Culture Survey was created to ask what employees see other employees do or what seems to be considered acceptable values and behaviors in their organization.

When you are working to improve security culture, you want the information you use to have the correct perspective. Knowledge and behaviors should be measured at an individual level to identify where weak spots and strong points are located. Sometimes there is an employee or group who has a specific behavior or lacks certain knowledge. Identifying those specific employees and groups will help you address problem areas as well as celebrate and reinforce strong areas.

In addition to gaining this knowledge about specific employees, you need to be able to zoom out. You want a broad perspective.

Culture is about the group, whereas individuals are part of the group. You can most accurately measure the group perspective by asking about people's observations and perceptions of the organization, not about what they (as individuals) know or do. You want to ask what employees see other employees do, not what they tell you they do themselves.

Compared to how you tackle knowledge and behaviors, working with culture requires a broader set of tools and controls. These would include tools often associated with organizational culture management, communication strategies, training, support teams, and even technology-based support tools. We'll discuss these strategies for influencing culture more in Chapters 8, 10, and 12.

Influencing culture is about understanding the interplay between the dimensions.

Influencing culture is about understanding the interplay between the dimensions.

And it's about understanding the interplay between people, process, and technology. Changing one facet will both directly and indirectly influence the other facets. You need to be aware of this. Understand where you

---

are and where you want to go. Build your hypothesis. Then test and measure your results.

Example Findings from Measuring the Seven Dimensions

Here are a couple findings from our recent research. Because we collect data using the same set of items across thousands of organizations around the world, we are able to understand regional differences in security.

Normalized Use of Unauthorized Services

Employee use of unauthorized services, often referred to as *shadow IT*, poses a threat to organizations on many levels. Traditionally, it has been difficult to measure this phenomenon, usually because employees are not very likely to admit to breaking the company rules. The Security Culture Survey circumvents this bias, giving us a unique peek into how large a problem shadow IT is.

As shown in Figure 6.2, employees report that unauthorized use of cloud services and file sharing services is considered normal by a minimum of 20 percent of employees, all the way up to 54 percent of employees in Asia. Depending on where your organization operates, between one in two and one in five employees consider it normal, and thus okay, to circumvent organizational security policies to get their job done. What security norms exist in your organization? How are those norms impacting your risk?

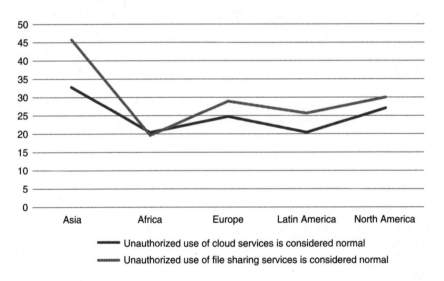

Figure 6.2   Use of shadow IT across regions

Confidentiality and Insider Threats

Here's another example. We wanted to study how well employees are able to determine what confidential information is in the context of their workplace. Our research shows that many employees do not know what is considered confidential information. As shown in Figure 6.3, this lack of understanding represents a serious insider threat, as between 20 percent and 40 percent of employees globally struggle to know what company confidential information is and what it is not.

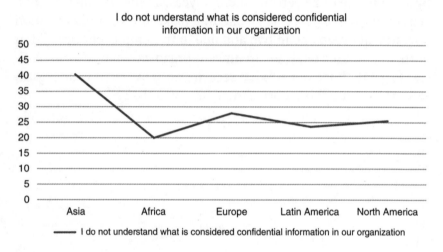

Figure 6.3 Employees struggle to properly classify information.

Understanding what is considered as confidential within an organization represents an issue within the *cognition* dimension of your security culture. You can address this via the dimension of *communication*. This can also be addressed by social modeling via *norms* and *responsibilities*.

Last Thought

By now, you can see that culture is something that can be demystified. It can be defined and measured. There's power in being able to do so. Understanding these dimensions of culture empowers us to uncover insights and useful facts about our organizations.

Takeaways

- Our working definition of culture is: *Security culture is the ideas, customs, and social behaviors of a group that influence its security.*
- A scientific understanding of security culture requires us to break culture down into measurable components. We call these the seven dimensions of security culture.
- The seven dimensions of security culture are: attitudes, behaviors, cognition, communication, compliance, norms, and responsibilities.
- Each dimension influences and is influenced by the other dimensions.
- Influencing culture is about understanding the interplay between the dimensions.

Chapter 7

Interviews with Organizational Culture Experts and Academics

The most important thing in science is not so much to obtain new facts as to discover new ways of thinking about them.

Sir William Bragg

As we were discussing the format of this book, one thing we really wanted to do was include the voices of several culture thought leaders. Notice we didn't say *security culture* thought leaders. We wanted to hear from academics, consultants, and practitioners who approach the topic of culture broadly. Our hypothesis is that, as you read our interviews with these experts, you'll actually learn quite a bit about security culture, because (after all) security culture is just another form of culture.

The format of this chapter is simple: We sent a list of seven questions to several thought leaders and asked each of them to (as their time allowed) complete at least four of the questions. This allowed each expert to focus on the questions they were most passionate about.

We asked the following questions:

- Why is culture important?
- Why do you find culture interesting?
- Is there a specific definition of culture that you find useful?
- How do you use metrics to improve culture / measure the effectiveness of cultural change?
- What actions can be taken to direct cultural change?
- Is there a success or horror story you'd like to share related to culture change? (Alternative question: What is your most interesting experience with culture?)
- How does a culture evolve (or how often?)

We hope you enjoy reading these interviews.

John R. Childress, PYXIS Culture Technologies Limited

- **Name:** John R. Childress
- **Title:** Chairman, PYXIS Culture Technologies Limited
- **Organization:** PYXIS Culture Technologies Limited

Why Is Culture Important?

I think culture's important because it matters, and it matters in a business sense. If you can think of culture as a business issue and not just an HR or an employee-engagement issue, you can see that it has a greater impact on all factors of the organization than just how people behave and how they think. It really has an impact on company value, profitability, customer loyalty, customer engagement. You just keep naming things, and there is a cultural imprint on all of those.

Why Do You Find Culture Interesting?

Every organization has a culture. Whether you want it or not, whether you desire it or not, whether it's by default, you're going to have a culture. And that culture is going to impact not only people's lives and the customer's lives, but the organization's life. So, I think culture is one of the most interesting and challenging areas that we can focus on.

Is There a Specific Definition of Culture That You Find Useful?

Culture is an ecosystem of organizational elements that influence and sustain employee behaviors in a predictable, certain way. And that ecosystem of cultural factors—I call them causal factors, or drivers—is how I define the culture. And the behavior is the output.

Culture really matters, but it's been hijacked by the HR behaviorists. And what I mean by that is, they only look at the individual behaviors and try and get a collective norm out of that, and say, "Well, that's the culture."

Employee behavior, which defines the culture, is just a visible output of the culture and not the culture itself. The culture is all those elements inside the organization. I call them drivers or causal factors. And if you can think of an ecosystem map or a root cause analysis map, you'll find a lot of drivers that create one or two outcomes. The same is true with culture. There are a lot of business elements inside the organization, like hiring profiles, onboarding, compensation, leadership style, supervision, policies, and internal work procedures. All those things interact and influence how people behave.

I think a great example is a compensation. If you look at banks, particularly the big banks, there's been several scandals and a huge number of fines for ethics and fraud violations. We don't hire fraudulent people, so what's going on? And what's going on is, there is a major driver within the banking culture, called excessive compensation and bonuses, which combined with a management focus on profitability versus customers or clients, you get a great forcing factor or a causal factor that causes people to cut corners. And cutting corners, often enough, leads to the next step. It's a slippery slope. And so, if we can see culture as an ecosystem of causal factors, then we can really understand why we have a culture the way we are and why people behave the way they behave.

What Actions Can Be Taken to Direct Cultural Change?

There are a series of steps. They don't all go linear, but they all work together. Number one is, you have to define your culture according to your business strategy. Your culture needs to support your business strategy. It's not an HR strategy. The best culture is the one that supports and promotes your business strategies. So, you really have to define what behaviors, what attitudes, what mindsets do we need in order to really drive our business strategy? That's number one.

Number two, then, is, you must map the culture. You have to determine what are the drivers of your current culture, what are causing.... And then you have to find the gaps between that culture that are going to support your strategy and your current culture. And there'll be some real strengths where they match perfectly, and there'll be some big gaps.

And then you need to look at it as a business problem and not just fixing people, because there are policies that drive unwanted behaviors; there are work processes that drive unwanted or unnecessary or unethical behaviors. And that's where leadership courage comes in and why it's a leadership problem. They have to step up and change those policies. And some of those policies have been around since the company began.

If you've got a model where you're able to get data into the causal factors, and you're able to continually stream data into those causal factors, and then you're able to link the causal factors with business outcomes, then you're measuring. I mean, you can't manage culture unless you measure it. You can't manage most things unless you measure them. And because culture's been hijacked by the behaviorists, it's always been this ephemeral set of metrics, which don't necessarily relate to actual business outcomes or even organizational inputs.

So, we need a robust model, a data-driven model, and then I think we can proactively manage culture, because if you have enough data and you have the right model, you can do predictive analysis. You could begin to see where some of these issues are, where people are ignoring policies that give us a cyber risk. Where are we hiring the wrong kinds of people, who created cyber risk? In other words, are we hiring thoughtful, risk-averse people, or are we hiring gung-ho break-the-rules-just-to-get-the-results kind of people?

And most organizations have not gone through that thought process.

Is There a Success or Horror Story You'd Like to Share Related to Culture Change?

A really good success story, which ties into my view of culture as an enterprise issue and a business issue, is the turnaround at Ford when Alan Mulally, who was a Boeing executive, not an auto man, was brought in. Ford was losing a billion five a month; it was a serious turnaround. And what he noticed about the leadership team is that they were very much silo-focused. They were really performing well on their individual functional objectives but sub-optimizing on the enterprise. And what he did is, he took away all their variable compensation based on functions and based on whatever else they had, and he put it all on the success of the enterprise; just a few metrics: sales, profitability, and growth. And now for everybody, that's all they got paid on. It totally turned around the mindset to where they realized that they had to start sharing information, sharing resources, and even sharing people.

As a result of that, there's an account of a guy who said, "I got this big opportunity in Europe, but I don't have enough trucks. I just don't have the inventory, and I can't build them fast enough. We could really help our overall sales goals if I could get these." And a couple people spoke up, "Well, I got 5,000 trucks in Turkey. And I got X number of trucks here and there, and I could ship them to you." That would've never happened in the old functional model.

And so, to me, that's one of those breakthrough changes that reset the organization's mindset about how they could work together and drive the business forward.

How Does a Culture Evolve (or How Often?)

Whenever people come together in an organization, you're going to have a culture. It's going to be weak at first, and then it's going to get stronger and stronger. And there are a couple ways that culture evolves. One is by leadership reinforcing it. So, if they ignore it, it will drift, and it will go to probably the lowest common denominator. If they are really serious about driving a culture that supports people and their strategy, then they're going to really reinforce it in every speech, every meeting, And so on.

Culture also drifts. Think of it like the concept of continental drift. Culture drifts in multiple ways. One is leadership ignoring it. Another is when there's a growth period and you hire a lot of people, but you don't enculturate them; you don't have the onboarding that is robust in what we believe and how we behave and what's good behavior, and what's not acceptable, etc. And if you don't have that, people are going to bring their own culture. They're going to bring the culture they're comfortable with, from their former company or whatever. And the third way is through M&A. And a lot of organizations grow through mergers and acquisitions, and they totally ignore the culture. That M&A move might be a good strategic fit, it might be a good financial fit, but is it a good cultural fit? You need to address all of those simultaneously.

Professor John McAlaney, Bournemouth University, UK

- **Name:** Professor John McAlaney
- **Title:** Professor in Psychology
- **Organization:** Bournemouth University, UK

Why Is Culture Important?

As humans we like to think of ourselves as being independent creatures that are in control of our own thoughts and behaviours. This is especially the case in many Western cultures, where there is an emphasis on individual success and wellbeing. However, the reality is that we are all influenced by the people around us, often to a far greater extent than we realise or perhaps want to admit. Understanding the influence of culture—be it on a national level or within an organization—is vital if we are able to predict and change individual behaviour.

Why Do You Find Culture Interesting?

Culture is interesting to me as a psychologist because it is so pervasive and influences so much of who we are and how we behave, yet most of the time we are oblivious to the impact it is having on us. It is also interesting because it is extremely complicated whilst also being something that everyone can relate to—if you talk about culture to an average employee in an organization, they understand what it is you are referring to. However, as soon as you start to try to deconstruct and quantify the components that make up culture, it becomes apparent that it is very difficult to do this.

Is There a Specific Definition of Culture That You Find Useful?

Defining culture is difficult and can vary depend on the context being discussed. For information security culture, I would say that the following definition by Da Veiga and Eloff (2010) is the most comprehensive:

"Attitudes, assumptions, beliefs, values and knowledge that employees/stakeholders use to interact with the organization's systems and procedures at any point in time. The interaction results in acceptable or unacceptable behavior (i.e., incidents) evident in artifacts and creations that become part of the way things are done in the organization to protect its information assets. This information security culture changes over time."

However, I do also like the simplicity of the definition by Lundy and Cowling (1996), who state that culture is *"the way things are done."*

What Actions Can Be Taken to Direct Cultural Change?

It is often commented that changing culture is very difficult. I would argue that it is quite easy to change culture—the difficult part is changing it in the direction that you desire. This is because culture is so complicated that it can be very difficult to predict what will happen if you attempt to alter it. Nevertheless, there is a wider evidence base around behaviour and culture change from psychological research that can be applied. It would require a lot of space to go into each of these in detail, but in brief—in [the] case of security within an organization—it involves making the expectations and requirements of the organization clear. It also involves ensuring that desired values and goals of the organization are visible at all levels of that organization. For example, if an organization may on paper and in staff training sessions proclaim that they value a good security culture, this could be completely undermined if the senior management behave in ways that do not align with this culture. In other words, for culture change to be successful within an organization it needs to be a genuine, authentic, and transparent effort by everyone in that organization.

Linked to the above, culture change also needs to consider the individual values and needs of the members of that culture. It is easy for management to say that a certain behaviour (for instance writing down passwords) should stop because it is bad practice, but they need to understand why that behaviour is happening in the first place. It could be that the socio-technical system that the organization uses inadvertently creates barriers that prevent employees from behaving in the ways that they know they should. This reflects the view within cybersecurity that humans are the weakest link—humans do indeed do a lot of irrational things, but often our behaviour represents our best effort to achieve what is expected of us in systems that are complicated, contradictory, and demanding.

To truly achieve positive and long-term culture change, it is very important to work with members of the culture to understand why they do what they do. Similarly, it is important to be realistic about how much emotional investment you can expect from employees. An employee working night shifts for minimum wage is unlikely to have the same level of buy-in to the security culture of an organization as a top executive on a high salary.

Is There a Success or Horror Story You'd Like to Share Related to Culture Change?

Alternative Question: What Is Your Most Interesting Experience with Culture?

There is an interesting story of how Arizona's Petrified Forest National Park attempted to stop tourists from taking home pieces of petrified wood as souvenirs. Initially signs were put up around the park that reported how much wood was being lost, and to ask visitors not to contribute to this problem—the result of which was that theft of the wood increased. This was because the signs that had been put up were unintentionally creating a perception amongst visitors that taking home souvenirs was the normal thing to do. To address this, new signs were put up, which stated that most visitors to the park do not take home souvenirs—i.e., that the culture was to leave the forest intact. The result of this new campaign was a marked drop in the amount of wood being taken from the park. I like this example because it demonstrated how a well-intended attempt to change culture backfired, and how something as simple as putting up signs can markedly change behaviour.

Additional details about this example are available at www .tandfonline.com/doi/full/10.1080/15534510500181459.

How Does a Culture Evolve (or How Often?)

Cultures continually evolve. Within an organization this evolution is due to several factors, such as changing business requirements, changing workforces, and changing demands. Organizational culture also sits within and is influenced by national culture—although

I would note that there is a surprising lack of research on the relationship between national culture and organizational culture. This is one of the reasons why applying culture change can be difficult and is why culture change must be an ongoing and adaptive process. It is not something that can be achieved once and then left alone.

Dejun "Tony" Kong, PhD, Muma College of Business, University of South Florida

- **Name:** Dejun "Tony" Kong, PhD
- **Title:** Associate Professor, Management; Faculty Director, Bishop Center for Ethical Leadership; Academic Director, Bachelor of Science in Management; Affiliate Faculty, Women's and Gender Studies
- **Organization:** Muma College of Business, University of South Florida

Why Is Culture Important?

Culture can influence people's personality, beliefs, values, perceptions, attitudes, emotions, behaviors, etc. Culture can help connect people and build strong groups but can also divide people and cause social conflict. Culture is everywhere, working to influence our life with or without our awareness.

Why Do You Find Culture Interesting?

Culture has always been fascinating to me. This topic is fascinating to many other social and behavioral scientists as well. I am always curious about why people who have different backgrounds think and behave differently, and how to enable people to be more cooperative and prosocial for collective prosperity. Cultural differences present opportunities for learning, creativity, and value creation, and yet people are anxious or even resistant to cultural differences and thus miss the opportunities for learning, creativity, and value creation. A good leader understands the importance and power of culture, and yet many leaders do not know how to be a good architect of culture.

Is There a Specific Definition of Culture That You Find Useful?

Hofstede and Hofstede (2005, p.28) defined culture as *"the collective programming of the mind which distinguishes the members of one group or category of people from another."*

How Do You Use Metrics to Improve Culture / Measure the Effectiveness of Cultural Change?

To me, the most critical metric for evaluating cultural change is trust. That's why I emphasize the central role of trust for ethical leadership in the Bishop Center for Ethical Leadership at the University of South Florida. Unfortunately, trust is declining over years in the U.S. society. Some recent thought of human resource management on organizational culture has considered trust to be essential for organizational culture above and beyond "positive culture." Are people capable of fulfilling their responsibilities and attaining goals? Are people benevolent to one another, instead of being selfish? Do people follow acceptable principles as a guide to their actions? Building trust is an effective and efficient way to promote cooperation and altruism.

Michael Leckie, Silverback Partners, LLC

- **Name:** Michael Leckie
- **Title:** Founding Partner
- **Organization:** Silverback Partners, LLC

Why Is Culture Important?

In order to answer the question of "why is culture important?" we need to first be clear on what we mean by culture. I always fall back on the groundbreaking work of Edgar Schein to understand the level of cultures; there are the visible artifacts of culture (how we dress, how our workplaces look, the common vocabulary, etc.); there are the stated values of a culture (those things we say that we are—the values we state are ours), and the tacit assumptions or how we believe things really work and what really matters. And, in that last level of culture, we find the heart of it. Culture is "how things really work around here" in an organization or social construct.

Culture is important because it is the context in which things get done (or don't, more to the point sometimes). This becomes critically important in understanding problems, overcoming struggles, and making progress. It becomes important because culture is the context or framework which defines competence. Let me say that again directly: Competence is cultural. You can be very good in your field of expertise, but if you cannot understand and adapt to the culture, you cannot be competent. It's easy to see this in more visible aspects of geopolitical cultures. Say, for example, you are a carnival barker or maybe an airplane pilot. Both very different roles. And let's say you are excellent at both. But if you try to do your job in Japan or in India, assuming you are Canadian or American carnival barker or airline pilot, you will struggle to be as competent. First of all, you don't speak the language, and so you have a hard time communicating and a hard time understanding the social signals you are receiving. Our Canadian carnival barker is going to have a real difficulty in convincing the Japanese, who don't understand him and whom he can't easily read the emotional reactions of, to come into the tent and see the show. The pilot is going to struggle to understand and be heard when she does not speak the language, and she might forget that some of her basic understanding and habits of flight are, quite literally, turned upside down. These challenges are obvious in my silly examples, but not so obvious when I move from PepsiCo to Coca-Cola as a marketer. But we've all experienced these situations where we move to a new job and we are a bit bewildered by what is going on, what people mean when they talk, what they don't talk about, where the "bombs" are and the things you need to avoid doing and saying, what people want to hear and see to believe you are competent. So, culture is critically important in understanding how to be effective and competent at what you are hired to do.

Why Do You Find Culture Interesting?

I find culture interesting because it is ubiquitous and yet mostly unseen and unacknowledged. It is just the way it is, and, therefore, we tend to attribute counter-cultural behavior to a lack in the person displaying those behaviors not to some aspect of "us" and the water we swim in. So, it is a hidden barrier and, conversely, a hidden opportunity to accelerate one's ability to impact others and be effective, if they can manage or master the culture quicker than others.

As humans, we crave certainty and safety as a matter of survival programmed into our brains through evolution. We also have a strong internal desire to belong, as a part of that safety and survival. Culture is where we find belonging and where we find the distinction from others that increases that safe feeling of belonging. As a result, we tend to overlook, and indeed unsee, the drawbacks to the culture(s) we live in. They're like family; they may be imperfect, but they are ours. Our culture and our context guide us in our choices and assumptions overwhelmingly, but we have talked about "culture" so much that it has become like the word "love"—used in such a broad set of definitions as to become almost meaningless. I "love" my wife and I "love" Thai food, but those are entirely different things. With this ubiquitous non-specificness, we lose sight of its impact on us and think we are making choices and operating from a place of clear-sighted rationality, not through a highly colored and specific cultural lens. The fact that culture has us flying a bit blind is what I find so interesting.

Is There a Specific Definition of Culture That You Find Useful?

"How things work around here" is probably the best and worst definition of culture. It is best because it is so accurate. Culture is the rules, mostly unwritten, of how things work or don't work (or are not allowed) in a given context or organization. But the phrase is so glib as to imply that it's not really worth digging deeper into the "why" of how things work and to potentially challenge how things work as the best way for them to work.

Most often, when not discussing culture in the more specific terms that thought leaders like Edgar Schein use, I rely on defining it starting from the individual. We all have values and assumptions (beliefs, sometimes hidden to others and ourselves) that guide our choices. When we have a group of people with some shared values (and beliefs) and some shared purpose, then we have a culture. Or, to simplify, culture is a group of individuals with enough shared values, beliefs, and purpose as to cohere.

How Do You Use Metrics to Improve Culture / Measure the Effectiveness of Cultural Change?

Using metrics with culture is a bit of a Holy Grail with consultants and OD practitioners. We have defaulted to using surveys of opinion, all of them highly colored by the underlying assumptions of their creators and, therefore, mostly directed and influenced opinion masquerading as data. Now, to be honest, there is a lot of "data" in organizations that is just that—opinion and propaganda disguised as truth or fact—and it can still be useful. But it tends to fall apart when the people with the purse strings start looking for "hard data" to base decisions on. They like hard data with credits and debits (themselves a form of fiction depending on the convoluted rules that financial people set up, but that's a rant for another time). But the question of actual return-on-investment metrics around culture is mostly conjecture.

I have had the privilege of working with one company's product that I think is making some useful connections in the worlds of data and culture. CEO George Swisher of changeforce.ai has a software tool that allows organizations to set goals and link the behavior changes that drive those goals to business systems and metrics a company measures. The logic thread that sets them apart is the simple connection of starting with strategic goals, breaking them down into behavioral pillars and drivers that we are reasonably certain will further those goals, and then continuously measuring the areas in the organization where those behaviors are changing (measured through the evaluation of all employees or participants), and then being able to slice and dice company metrics along the lines of where behaviors are changing and where they are not. Partnering with George and his team to use my own set of Change-Able attributes has allowed me to put forward a much more robust, and far less manipulable, set of data about actual change (in behaviors) and business outcomes.

What Actions Can Be Taken to Direct Cultural Change?

Directing cultural change is difficult, very difficult. But maybe not difficult for the reasons we would immediately think. It is not actually that difficult to understand and there is a very simple key to doing it, but we find it very hard to use that key because it is, well, often very counter-cultural. So, let's start there. Culture is hard to change because culture is us. If culture is a group of individuals with enough shared values, beliefs, and purpose as to cohere, then that means that we are working against our own values and beliefs (or assumptions, sometimes hidden to others as well as ourselves) in order to change it. So, tell me: When was the last time you actually changed a belief? And I am talking about beliefs, not opinions. Not when you met someone and were unsure about them but then found out they shared your favorite movie and liked your fave bands and were politically aligned, so you decided that they were kind of OK after all? No, I am talking about a belief: What's a sin or immoral?; does God exist and which one is the real one?; how do you talk to and treat others?; who matters more in this world? Face it, we all have a set of assumptions about what is right and wrong that rarely change and, if they do, not usually without some real soul-searching, maybe some trauma, and *not without finding a new set of people who also believe in the new thing [we] now believe in.*

And this moves us into the second tricky part of changing beliefs (in order to change culture): Not only are we working against ourselves, but we are also working against our tribe. Changing beliefs is something that we just don't do on our own. We need help; we need influence; and we need a new place to belong. This is why people join an organization and they adapt to the culture, not change it (except in rare circumstances).

Finally, culture shows up, most often, in the conversations we have. Culture is dialogue-driven. What we say (and don't say) and how we say it, and who says what, is where culture is observed, activated, and reinforced. And those are our levers: individual change, within a group, driven by dialogue.

Realizing all that, we now know we need to focus on individual change, and starting to build a tribe within the culture we are hoping to direct change in. I often say to my clients (to their annoyance I can imagine) that "you change culture by changing culture." What I mean by that is that we need to introduce a new dialogue, person-by-person, in a group in order to manifest change in small, somewhat contained, bits of the organization. Once things start to change with the individuals and the group, the new culture begins to take hold. Once enough of those "bits" change, the viral momentum takes hold, and the change begins to drive and accelerate.

The last bit of the puzzle is the new dialogue. What does that mean? Here is where we most often get it wrong. We start by just asking people to state new beliefs or values as if they believe them, which they don't. No, the value of dialogue not in just parroting corporate change propaganda; it is in turning dialogue into behavior, and that means questions, not statements, not answers. Asking a question that we might not normally ask, a counter-cultural question, is a behavior. The act of asking the counter-cultural question (and the answering and learning from that act) introduces new culture into a group. The key to directing cultural change is individually, in groups, through counter-cultural questions.

Is There a Success or Horror Story You'd Like to Share Related to Culture Change?

Alternative Question: What Is Your Most Interesting Experience with Culture?

The greatest success story of culture change I know is from an organization that used to be known as Abitibi-Price. They have gone through tremendous industry consolidation (the newsprint industry) and evolutions and are an entirely different company now. But at the time, the largest producer of papers for communication in the world was a tremendous culture change success story. Most of that can be attributed to the leadership of Ron Oberlander, the CEO. Ron has, sadly, passed away from cancer [. . .] but he still stands out as maybe the best CEO I have ever seen (and I have seen a lot of CEOs). Ron knew intuitively that he had to change the conversations and that this meant starting with himself. He also knew that a vision or stated values were useless unless he lived them first, publicly, and vulnerably. So, he created a framework for dialogue simply based on "how is this (decision, action, etc.) living our values?" He drove this conversation by having it constantly and by making sure he was questioned first and publicly. He made it safe for others to have that conversation. There was much more that Ron did to lead this work, but that was the core. The result was industry-leading business outcomes through the creation of a culture that allowed a global company to operate as one in the values-based decisions and actions they took and a workforce that was relentless in improvement. A great leader does not "direct" change—they live it. And they live it first, and they live it publicly. And that is probably the single biggest impediment to culture change in modern organizations. Is leadership willing to lead by example, not by mandate?

How Does a Culture Evolve (or How Often?)

Culture evolves constantly. The more interesting question, to me, is how often does it evolve intentionally and for the better? Culture evolves as the individuals that comprise the culture change or enter and leave. But this happens slowly and over time, even if constantly. There can be big jolts to culture when there is a large turnover in people, a coming together of entities, or major changes in leadership. But this is rarely intentional. We often state that we are bringing in new leadership to change culture, but two things must line up for this to work. First, the culture itself must be negatively impacting the business entity. There must be a strain produced by the culture no longer being strategically appropriate or adaptive (to use Kotter's terms). Second, the new leadership must truly believe that changing culture is their number one job. We have seen evidence of this in Microsoft under Satya Nadella. The combination of business struggles and Nadella's unwavering belief that culture was critical (and needed changing) and his personal efforts to drive that change, starting with himself and his leadership team, was what made the culture change happen to the extent it has out in Redmond, WA.

So, yes, culture does evolve and constantly, but this is often not as planned or needed without the right circumstances and the right leadership.

Part III

Transformation

This is where the rubber meets the road. In Part III, we introduce multiple tools for measuring and influencing your security culture. We discuss how each dimension of security culture interacts with the whole, explore sticking points, and help you build your security culture program. We close out this part with some tips for gaining and maintaining executive support and then provide a number of interviews with security culture thought leaders.

Chapter 12: Planning and Maturing Your Program
Chapter 13: Quick Tips for Gaining and Maintaining Support
Chapter 14: Interviews with Security Culture Thought Leaders
Chapter 15: Parting Thoughts

Chapter 8
Introducing the Security Culture Framework

You don't have to be a genius or a visionary or even a college graduate to be successful. You just need a framework and a dream.

Michael Dell

The Security Culture Framework was developed by Kai Roer, this book's coauthor, in 2010–2011. Kai had been providing security consulting services for nearly two decades; for several years he noticed that a critical area was being neglected: the human layer. At that time, the only nod to the importance of human factors was (with few exceptions) very boring security awareness training. These early training programs tended to focus on giving people tons of information while also making them feel bad or scared because they can be the cause of so many problems.

The missing piece of the puzzle was the understanding that humans, our coworkers, can be an asset to our cybersecurity programs—an asset that should be equipped and mobilized.

The missing piece of the puzzle was the understanding that humans, our coworkers, can be an asset to our cybersecurity programs—an asset that should be equipped and mobilized.

But there was a challenge. No structured approach existed, and little scientific evidence of which types of approaches produce meaningful results was available.

During that time, Kai was consulting with several organizations from all around the world, ranging from large retail organizations in the Nordics to defense sectors in Western countries, to some of the largest telecom providers in the world. They all shared a similar question: How do we engage our people to better secure our information? In 2010, that repeated question set Kai on a quest to create a methodology that could be easily communicated and adopted by organizations around the world. This had to be a scalable, repeatable process that could be understood and adopted by the global security community. A year later, the Security Culture Framework was born and published under the Creative Commons license.

Within a very short time, organizations all around the world— from the Navy in Australia to the Navy in Norway—began adopting the Security Culture Framework. It was being taught in MBA classes and recommended by ENISA, the European Union Agency for Cybersecurity. It also had the side effect of igniting a global interest in the topic of security culture.

Figure 8.1 depicts the Security Culture Framework in its simplest form. The Security Culture Framework is lean and deceptively simple. Think of it as a virtuous cycle consisting of a few simple steps to be completed in sequence: *measure*, *involve*, and *engage*. Each step has specific tasks that result in output, which is then fed into the next step. After one full cycle, the expectation is that you will be able to document change—preferably improvements.

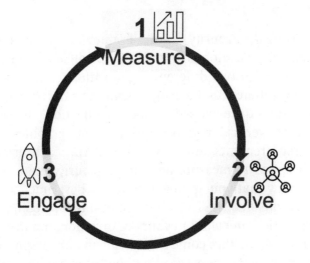

Figure 8.1 The Security Culture Framework at a glance

Commit for the Long Haul

The key to any *process* is to realize that it is not to be treated as a *project*. It is not a one-and-done event or set of events. It is a *program* that, once put in place, should run continuously, stopping only if being replaced in the future by a better, more effective process.

The Power of Three

The Security Culture Framework consists of three steps: *measure*, *involve*, and *engage*. We provide an overview of each step in this chapter. Be sure to check out the resource website for this book for additional information, worksheets, and more.

When using the Security Culture Framework, keep in mind that each organization is unique. There will always be similarities between two different organizations, but there are also many differences. Each organization has its own unique culture—a culture shaped by the organization's founders, its industry vertical, region, employee demographics, regulatory requirements, and much more. Approach any process designed to measure and shape security culture in a similar way that you approach industry best practices and certifications like NIST or ISO. The best results come from adapting the framework to your organization, not the other way around. In this context, that means answering each question by using your specific knowledge and experience from your organization.

Step 1: Measure

The first step in the process is *measure*. We use the term broadly to include:

- The act of measuring
- The use of a set of specific measurement targets (metrics)
- The act of analyzing the results of the measurements

This step also includes setting goals for your security culture and identifying the deltas between the current culture and what you want to achieve.

Measuring culture can be a daunting task. You probably already have access to a wide range of tools that can be used to measure culture, including workplace engagement tools, survey tools, focus groups, management consultants, and more. But the critical question will always be whether you are measuring the right aspects of culture and if the tool(s) and questions you've selected for the task are effective.

The good news is that measuring culture isn't something new. Humans have been measuring various aspects of culture for at least two millennia. We could fill entire libraries with the observations about humans and human nature written by philosophers, poets, medical professionals, theologians, and anthropologists.

No matter how you choose to define your metrics, you need to be reasonably certain that they measure security culture, and that you can repeat the same (not just similar) measurements again after each full iteration of the process. If you are struggling to find such metrics, we suggest our previously discussed Seven Dimensions of Security Culture.

For now, let's discuss the three actions to take in the measure step. As shown in Figure 8.2, these subactions are:

1. Know where you are.
2. Decide where you want to be.
3. Find your gap.

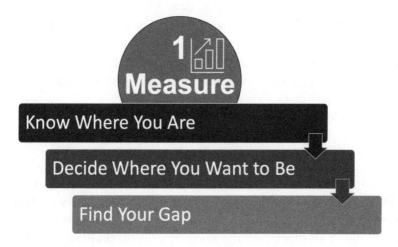

Figure 8.2 Step 1: Measure

Know Where You are

If you don't know where you are, you'll never know how far you've come or how far you have yet to go. As such, the first action is to define your current baseline. This baseline is a moving target; it will be updated at each iteration of the process. The purpose of the baseline is to have a clear understanding of your current status, your status quo. In ISO, this is sometimes called the *as-is state*. The baseline is later used in the gap analysis and revisited every iteration of the process.

Your first time using the Security Culture Framework, you'll begin measuring with a clean slate. Spend some time deciding which measurements and metrics you want to apply in the process of improving your security culture. Chapter 9, "The Secrets to Measuring Security Culture," is dedicated to measuring culture, so we've got you covered there if you don't already have an idea of the culture aspects you want to measure. Ensure that you'll be able to measure the same phenomena with the same tool throughout multiple iterations of the process. The metrics you choose are often dependent on what kind of data and tools you have available. Find measurements that can be repeated, are not biased, and will likely also be relevant 5 to 10 years from now.

Remember, this is a cyclical process. Set time frames for subsequent measurements, using the same tools and collecting the same metrics you measured previously. Update the tracking system you have put in place so that you can follow your progress across multiple iterations.

After you know where you are you're ready to. . .

Decide Where You Want to Be

The future status is your goal state, often referred to as the *to-be state* by ISO. This is the state you want your security culture to achieve across each metric you measure. The goal is used to steer your actions and focus on the security culture program in general, and more specifically the actions and choices you make during each iteration. You will also use your goals in your communication with stakeholders, especially in the *involve* step.

We recommend setting three levels of goals:

- A long-term goal (possibly 3–5 years)
- An intermediary goal (such as 12–24 months)
- A per-iteration goal

Align your long-term goals to the organization's vision and high-level direction. For example, an insurance company that contracted Kai to help establish its security culture management program ultimately selected its 5-year business goals, including customer satisfaction drivers, to inform its 5-year security culture goals. The benefits of tying your security program directly to business targets and long-term goals are substantial: direct engagement with the executives, expenses aligned with business focus, and easy communication using business language that everyone understands. In other words, this type of alignment makes the security culture program a business focus and helps executives understand the program's relevance.

Long-term goals are strategic and can often feel aspirational. That's where iterative goals help. You've undoubtedly heard the rhetorical question and answer set, *"How do you eat an elephant? One bite at a time."* That's where iterative goals come in. They are the series of single bites that you use to achieve your larger goals. Iterative goals are designed be attainable and help you make progress. Don't be afraid to add stretch goals: goals that you aren't entirely sure that you will be able to reach. No matter what, you'll learn something by working toward them. These kinds of goals can be used to understand if certain training content resonates with a specific segment of your employee population, or if some behaviors are more likely in certain areas. The point is to uncover things you can use to improve your security program across all areas of people, process, policy, and technology.

With short-term goals, the focus is to define goals and targets for this specific iteration of the program. Many times, these short-term goals can seem obvious. They are progressive steps needed to achieve your midterm or long-term goals. Resist the urge to get tunnel vision here. Dig deeper. Ask yourself: In order to get to our 5-year goal, what do we need to do today? This month? This quarter? This year? When you do this thoroughly, you may even surprise yourself by uncovering some non-obvious goals and steps to achieve those goals.

Dig deeper. Ask yourself: In order to get to our 5-year goal, what do we need to do today? This month? This quarter? This year? When you do this thoroughly, you may even surprise yourself by uncovering some non-obvious goals and steps to achieve those goals.

Break down each goal and match it with at least one metric to measure progress. See Chapter 9 for more information.

It is better to set one single goal and run an iteration than to define too many metrics and goals. Keep it simple, especially in the beginning. You can always expand as you learn more.

Once you have a list of goals and proposed metrics, it is time to move to the gap analysis phase.

Find Your Gap

The final phase in the *measure* step is to compare your baseline with your goal state. If you have both iterative and long-term goals, consider the long-term goals and their distance from the baseline.

Your focus, however, should be on the iterative goals. The purpose of this stage is to get a clear idea of how far away you are from your next goal. For example, if your baseline is that 30 percent of employees currently click phishing simulations and your goal is to get that to under 4 percent, then the gap is clear: from 30 percent to 4 percent. Now comes the bigger question: *Is it realistic to reach that goal in this iteration?* If not, then you need to set a new goal (something between 30 percent and 4 percent) for your next iteration. No matter what, you need to make a deliberate decision and record your rationale and any additional information and/or ideas that will help you achieve the goal.

When you believe you've set reasonable goals that can be achieved within the target iteration time frame, it's time to move to the *involve* step of the framework.

Analyzing Your Results

At the end of each iteration of the Security Culture Framework, it's time to see how far you've come. Use the same measurement tools and metrics you used when creating your baseline to perform a new measurement. When the new numbers are in, compare them with the following:

- **Your baseline numbers:** What was the change between your baseline and now? Was the change positive or negative? Did some areas change more rapidly than others? Can you determine the root cause for any unexpected outcomes?
- **Your future status:** Did you achieve your goals yet? How far away are you? Do you see areas that did not improve? Areas that showed degression?
- **Your actions taken in the *involve* and *engage* steps:** Are there specific actions taken that had a more positive or negative impact than anticipated? Are there areas

(continued)

(continued)

where you lack data and measurement capabilities? Are there areas you are currently measuring that aren't producing valuable insights? Which actions should be repeated, refreshed, or removed?

Make notes on what you learned in this iteration as well as what you would like to change, improve, and remove.

This is also a good time to update a trend chart and add your new baseline to any spreadsheets or tools you're using to track progress. Include all supporting data you find useful, such as the future status you had for this iteration, date, link to decisions you made in the *involve* and *engage* steps, and other program-related notes. Tracking and reporting over time is the only way to see where you began, how far you've come, and how far you still must go. Seeing your progress can be encouraging to you and your team, and your progress charts can be a key ingredient in keeping buy-in throughout your program.

Step 2: Involve

The second step in the Security Culture Framework is *involve* (see Figure 8.3). This step is all about building support with key stakeholders and understanding how different employees may require different approaches to generate desired security-related outcomes. Many organizations also use this stage to identify security culture carriers (also known as ambassadors, champions, influencers, etc.). These culture carriers may take on a wide variety of tasks and responsibilities. Their ultimate purpose is to help facilitate communication, reflect security values, help establish and motivate peer groups, and more.

Building Support

No matter where your organization is today, you can take steps to build and manage security culture starting right now. But this is a journey that's much easier to take with support from above. That may involve evolving your language from security to risk. Risk management is often a critical part of any organization, and many leaders speak and think in risk-based terms and scenarios.

Figure 8.3   Step 2: Involve

One effective way to gain support is by providing evidence and through storytelling. If you are wondering how to gain support for your security culture program, approach your executives and board with facts and scenarios that tell stories about risk, especially if these stories relate to similar organizations.

Approach your executives and board with facts and scenarios that tell stories about risk, especially if these stories relate to similar organizations.

There is no shortage of research, articles, and presentations that can help you assemble the evidence and stories you need. For instance, the cybersecurity industry produces some great material, including the annual Verizon DBIR, IBM's annual Cost of a Data Breach Report, and the annual Security Culture Report by KnowBe4 Research. These reports, and many others, share important data that security leaders, business executives, and boards of directors are using to understand their risk profile and how they are doing compared to other organizations.

A benefit of the first step in the Security Culture Framework, *measure*, is that you are collecting data yourself. In addition to ensuring that the program is on track, this data should be used to report progress and demonstrate the need of the program itself. By aligning your goals with those of the business, you are demonstrating how the security culture program is supporting the business and how it can be a key component to reducing human-based risk across the organization.

Different Audiences

Organizations come in all shapes and sizes. The same can be said about their employees. Some are enthusiastic; some are considerate. Some work with sales; some with engineering. Some are engaged in company secrets; some are not. You get the idea: Employees are different and have different security- and risk-related knowledge, beliefs, values, behavior patterns, expectations, and more. They each have different jobs and different exposure to information and threats. As a result, employees should be treated as individuals, not as one single mass. To be clear: Security programs must adhere to the needs of the single employee, which is the opposite of an annual compliance training forced upon every employee.

To be clear: Security programs must adhere to the needs of the single employee, which is the opposite of an annual compliance training forced upon every employee.

Yes, there may still be some required training that everyone must sit through because of compliance. Everything else? Adjust to the need of the employee.

Here's a quick example. One organization we worked with measured the security culture of its employees and discovered that approximately 20 percent (500) of its employees reported poor behavior on password hygiene. It used this knowledge to set up a security culture program specifically for those 500 employees. The rest of the workforce followed the normal security culture program. The result was great: In October 2021, one year after the program ended, these 500 employees showed significant improvement.

You may choose one or many target audiences per iteration. Use your goals for the iteration to select the employees to include or exclude. Once you have identified the target audience for this iteration, you are ready to move to the next step.

Step 3: Engage

This is where the fun happens. As shown in Figure 8.4, the *engage* step is all about the different activities and content you set up and distribute to your selected groups of employees. Select each goal from the *measure* step and the target audience from the *involve* step, and then decide which activities and topics the employees should be exposed to.

Figure 8.4   Step 3: Engage

Activities can be anything—they just need to be security- and risk-related. Here are a few examples:

- Phishing assessments
- E-learning
- Lunch-and-learns
- Live demonstrations
- Videos
- Group meetings

- Events
- Games
- Posters
- Newsletters
- Giveaways
- Surveys
- Dedicated Slack channels
- Text message reminders
- And more

You may ask how surveys or Slack channels can be considered activities. Here's where we come to a central truth of culture engagement. You are always teaching even when you aren't formally teaching, and people are always learning even when they aren't formally engaging in traditional learning processes. You are always setting the tone and providing examples that help with formal knowledge acquisition; however, perhaps even more importantly, you are helping to establish the unwritten rules, values, and behavior patterns that are *caught* rather than *taught*.

Always Teaching, Always Learning

Shouldn't all activities revolve around teaching? Our answer is that *everything* is teaching. Even things that you might consider as passive activities where your employees are giving you data can be used to teach them in the moment.

Consider something like a survey. We generally think of surveys as activities where employees share their thoughts, opinions, and feelings. But here's the cool part: Something as simple as survey questions can serve to engage your people. Simply presenting your employees the survey questions gets them thinking about the topics you are asking them about. Suddenly they are spending a few moments contemplating topics like password security, tailgating, secure document destruction, incident reporting, and more.

That kind of cognitive activity has been shown to influence ideas and behavior to such a degree that psychologists struggle to create surveys and experiments without influencing the mind of their subject. Thankfully, from a security perspective, our focus is to influence their minds and shape their behavior. When deployed purposefully, there are nearly limitless avenues to help drive security awareness, behavior, and culture.

We recommend that you use automated tools wherever possible. There are a number of tools that, when set up correctly, can help you gather measurements, identify target audiences, and distribute the right kind of content and activities to your employees. As of now, various aspects of these capabilities can be found in security awareness and training platforms, some human resources systems, learning experience platforms, survey creation tools, and other employee engagement systems. As the security awareness industry evolves, expect products within this category to gain significant functionality around culture management.

Rinse and Repeat

Anything worth doing once is worth doing again, right? When you've completed step three (engage), it is time to go back to step one (measure), then step two (involve) again, and, finally, step three (engage) again. It's a process.

Benefits of Using the Security Culture Framework

The main benefit of using the Security Culture Framework is to reduce risk and improve security. The framework is a process that is easy to implement and flexible enough to adjust to the changing needs in a security culture program. This flexibility means that organizations of any size can use it, and as organizations grow, the framework adopts.

Another benefit of using the framework is the documentation of status, progress, and change. In the case of a breach, some insurers and legislators may require that you have taken reasonable steps to prevent the event. Your process documentation can be used to prove to the board, stakeholders, auditors, and regulators that your program has taken due diligence steps to address the human layer, and that you've established processes and procedures designed and implemented to reduce risk and improve security.

This documentation has helped many auditors, both internal and external, to complete their work faster and with better results. Because the Security Culture Framework adheres to the same general principles of the ISO standards, if you have pursued an ISO 27000 process, you can reuse this already existing knowledge in your organization.

Applying the same process each time will reduce the overhead of your security culture program. Instead of reinventing the wheel every single time, you now know which parts are effective, which can be improved, and where you can learn. In the end, it is all about learning and applying that knowledge.

Takeaways

- The Security Culture Framework is a process consisting of three steps: *measure*, *involve*, and *engage*.
- It's all about setting goals and iterating through the process steps to move toward your goals.
- The best results come from adapting the framework to your organization, not the other way around.
- The best way to position your program for executives and boards is to use the language of risk.
- No matter what you are doing, you are always teaching, and your employees are always learning.

Chapter 9
The Secrets to Measuring Security Culture

To measure is to know. If you cannot measure it, you cannot improve it.

Lord Kelvin

Let's face it: It's hard to know how effective any program is at achieving its desired results unless you've established a set of objective measures. You need to know where you are doing well, where you aren't quite having the impact you want, and where you might be doing more harm than good. As Lord Kelvin said, "To measure is to know." But how do you measure awareness, behaviors, and culture? Great question. Glad you asked. In this chapter we describe our quest to accurately measure culture and how Kai and his team developed and refined the Security Culture Survey. Since its creation, this tool has been used by thousands of organizations to collect over a million survey responses, yielding the world's largest security-culture–related dataset.

In our experience, the most effective and accurate way to measure security culture is to administer the Security Culture Survey to all employees. The Security Culture Survey was developed and refined over years, based on research and strong academic principles. It has only one job: to measure security culture—nothing more, nothing less. The Security Culture Survey and reporting functions have been fully integrated into KnowBe4's security awareness and training platform and is available in many languages, making it easy to use for organizations worldwide. Yes, the full Security Culture Survey is part of a commercial offering, but it is not the only way to measure culture. You can begin measuring culture today regardless of the security awareness platform you use, and even if you don't currently use a security awareness vendor.

The Security Culture Survey: A History

The Security Culture Survey was created in 2015 by Kai Roer and Dr. Gregor Petrič. Their goal was to create a scientifically accurate means to measure the security-related aspects of a culture. A central requirement was that the tool had to be something that organizations could easily adopt. It needed to be quick to complete, easy to administer, and generate relevant and meaningful reports.

Analyzing the currently available research and practices, the team concluded that a survey was the best instrument. They began by creating an initial pool of almost 150 items that would measure security culture across 7 dimensions (attitudes, behaviors, cognition, communications, compliance, norms, and responsibilities).

Now here's the thing: Researchers love swimming in lots of data. They are data hungry. That's why this initial version of the survey included so many questions. From a research perspective, more survey questions mean more details; and more details equal more insights. From a practitioner perspective, however, more survey questions result in a greater burden for the person taking the survey, more time investment, and greater pushback from the organization.

To be a truly useful tool that could be readily adopted by organizations around the world, the 150 items had to be dramatically reduced. A review of the initial pool was done by several industry experts, resulting in a reduced pool of 96 items. This pool was then used to gather data from employees at an organization in Norway. Kai and his team reviewed the data and, as a result, determined that they could reduce the number of items to 72 and analyze for further efficiencies. That got them down to a pool of 42 items proven to accurately measure security culture across the 7 dimensions.

With the 42 items, it was time to distribute the survey more broadly. Over the next two years, more than 12,000 employees used the survey annually, allowing the team to gather enough data to determine which survey items were the key, critical questions that get to the heart of the 7 dimensions of security culture. That analysis yielded the needed information, allowing the team to reduce the survey to a set of 28 items.

The goal was met. The current version of the Security Culture Survey consists of 28 questions, takes less than 4 minutes to complete, and is currently the most widely used and accurate method for measuring security culture.

Connecting Awareness, Behavior, and Culture

In late 2021, our team at KnowBe4 Research kicked off a project to examine relationships that may exist between awareness, behavior, and culture. That project is still in its early stages, but we can already share some interesting high-level discoveries. For example, we have correlations showing that *knowledge* (general awareness) has a positive influence on the employee *behavior* of reporting phishing emails. This demonstrates that there is a connection between awareness and behaviors. Employees who have been trained how to identify phishing emails report them more often than those who have not received such training. A similar pattern is seen when employees click phishing links. The more knowledge they have, the less they click.

How Can You Measure the Unseen?

As discussed in Part I of this book, it is difficult to objectively observe any culture of which we are a part. We don't see it clearly, and there are several aspects, such as the unwritten rules of our own culture, that we just forget about. We take our own cultural environment for granted.

Observing some of the distinctions within other cultures is usually pretty easy for us—we quickly pick out those things that are different from our own ways. You can use this realization when measuring culture—for example, by observing the culture you currently have in your organization from an outside perspective. That may involve using outside consultants, holding focus groups, deploying surveys designed by third parties, interviewing new employees regarding what they notice about the organization's culture, and even interviewing long-time employees about their assumptions and experiences. All of this can help you obtain much needed perspective. It's about uncovering your blind spots, as well as gaps between what you currently have and what you want.

Using Existing Data

Many organizations collect large amounts of data—data that can be used to describe elements of culture. One example is incident reporting. Are employees reporting incidents or not? If they are reporting, and their reporting is relatively accurate, you can deduce that they are able to correctly identify potential incidents apart from something that is not. It may also indicate that they care enough to report it.

Be careful how you interpret your data. Just because incident reporting may indicate that someone has sufficient knowledge and that they care, the converse may not be true.

Just because incident reporting may indicate that someone has sufficient knowledge and that they care, the converse may not be true.

There can be myriad reasons why someone might not report an incident. For example, someone working in a low-conflict culture where employees avoid confrontations may choose not to report an incident because it might violate their perceived cultural codes. You may discover that in the United States or Europe, incidents are being reported, but in Southeast Asia fewer incidents are being reported even if incidents are clearly occurring.

A Data Dilemma

One challenge with measuring culture is not the lack of data but the choice of data. This may seem like an obvious statement, but here goes: If you want to measure behaviors, use data that specifically maps to the behaviors you are interested in. You can think about this from two different directions. First, consider the behaviors that are most important to you—for example, phishing, incident reporting, tailgating, password hygiene, and so on. Now, try to catalog the data you have available that provides evidence of that behavior. You should be able to quickly assemble a list of potential sources: phishing assessments, reported phishing

(continued)

(continued)

activities, training completions, resetting employee credentials, support requests and types, reported incidents and types, and more.

You can also find interesting data and behavior sources by working from the opposite direction. Create a catalog of the systems you have and the data these systems are able to report. These data sources can range from security-centric systems, such as security information and event management (SIEM) and data leak prevention (DLP) systems, to network infrastructure systems, such as web proxy logs, or even things more associated with employee interactions with the physical environment, like employee badge access systems. You'll quickly discover that many systems report data that can be associated with some form of user behavior, either directly or through inference. To be clear—we aren't fans of simply reporting something because you have the data, so don't let the tail wag the dog. But you never know—doing this kind of bottom-up analysis might yield some insights that are worth your attention.

There is also a large amount of data that may not be helpful when measuring culture. Most data will tell only part of the story. And data absent of context can be difficult to interpret correctly. Training completions, for example, can be a challenge. If you have low training-completion ratios, is that because of poor security culture, or is it because the training content or platform is outdated and difficult to use? Even if you have very high completion rates, what does that say about security culture? As it turns out, not much at all. Yes, it tells you that employees complete their assigned trainings, but not why they do it.

The Right Way to Use Data

A thoughtful analysis of culture requires more than just comparing scores and datasets across teams and locations. The culture you measure doesn't live in a black box; it is greatly influenced by a host of factors that you may not think to consider. Because of this, it can be difficult to make hard conclusions without digging deeper.

The culture you measure doesn't live in a black box; it is greatly influenced by a host of factors that you may not think to consider.

Remember our earlier example where some regional social customs may cause employees to be hesitant to report incidents? It's critical to understanding why some groups of employees may behave differently from others. In today's global workplace, where one team can consist of many different nationalities and cultures, it is even more important to dig deep when looking at discrepancies in the numbers—to find the why.

We encourage the use of interviews to gather more information when needed. An interview is a technique often applied in social science to uncover information that may be difficult to find through other means. Sometimes interviews will not be enough. There could be other, deeper culture-related aspects that are difficult to detect or articulate without proper experience and expertise. If you think that is possible in your organization, we recommend consulting with a cultural expert.

Methods of Measuring Culture

Culture can be measured any number of ways. Academics have successfully applied observation, experimentation, and interrogation (surveys and interviews) to measure culture. You can do the same.

Observation

Observation is the act of watching an individual or a group with the aim to understand. The purpose is not to make judgments but simply to monitor and learn what you can. You can use this technique to identify patterns and behaviors. For example:

- **Clean desks:** Do employees follow the clean desk policy? Often, it will be enough to walk around the office every now and then to make this observation. Do employees lock their screens when they leave their computer?
- **Tailgating:** Do employees let others into the office, even if it is against policy? This is also easy to observe. Just have someone stand near the entrance to your office in the morning, after lunch breaks, or at odd times of the day and record the behavior patterns they see. Don't forget to do the same type of observation for employee-only entrances near break areas (such as smoking areas or outdoor break areas). You may also use video recordings if the entrance has surveillance installed.
- **Email hygiene:** Most of us spend several hours each day inside our email inboxes. Is it normal to send jokes and memes by email? Is it common to drop links to non-work-related sites? Do your employees overshare sensitive information to large groups of people via email? For example, do they email groups of customers and expose customer email addresses to each other, or have they adopted the habit of using BCC to help protect customer privacy? You can also use email filtering tools to look for these patterns.

Observations are great for collecting limited amounts of data. It is often difficult to scale observations, and it can also be difficult to compare results over time and across locations unless you implement a formal system to record the observations. The use of a form, collecting key findings on a specific set of observations, and saving the data in a spreadsheet makes it easy to revisit and compare observations over time.

Experimentation

Experimentation is a common method of understanding behavior. Often used in psychology, experimentation can also be applied in business when we want to examine specific behaviors. One area that uses the experimentation technique is in phishing assessments. The experiment is simple: To what extent will the recipient be able to tell the test email from a legitimate email? In its simplest form, this experiment can be run by asking employees to report phishing emails. This will tell you if people are able to identify some phishing emails, but it leaves a lot unclear. A better method is to use a phishing assessment tool to schedule specific phishing emails to be sent to specific employees, and then monitor the employees' actions: Did they open the emails? Did they click a link? Did they share credentials? Did they report it? You may even check if they reported before or after some of the other actions.

A Fun Experiment

You can use experimentation on any number of behaviors you are interested in measuring. Here's a powerful (and fun) experiment that also serves as a great learning experience for the employee. Set up a password cracking unit during a lunchbreak or as a special event. Ask employees to enter their passwords (or sample passwords) and let them see how long it takes before their passwords are cracked. Our minds remember these types of real-world experiences and demonstrations much more readily than a boring PowerPoint presentation.

Interrogation (Surveys and Interviews)

A great way to gather information is by asking employees questions. This can be done informally, over lunch or in quick hallway conversations. Or it can be done more formally with an interview or survey consisting of prewritten questions designed to elicit open-ended answers or asking employees to choose the most accurate answer from a multiple choice set. Both methods can yield important and valuable information. Interviews, as opposed to surveys, are often most useful when you need to uncover specific information or when the information needed is best captured in an open, explorative dialogue. The downside of interviews, however, is that they don't scale well. They take significant planning, effort, and time.

Surveys are a solution to the scalability issue. With today's technology, creating, distributing, and analyzing data using surveys is cheap and fast—so cheap and fast that organizations may be tempted to overuse surveys, and employees are suffering under the weight of the number of surveys their organization asks them to complete each month. Another challenge with many surveys is that they are created without an understanding of how to craft questions and answer alternatives that will remove bias. Creating good survey items is an acquired skill and is not something that should be done without training. The same is true for the statistical skills required to correctly interpret the results.

A/B Testing

Measuring is also a tactical skill. Knowing the content type or topics that will generate the best results in your organization can be difficult. With so much great awareness training content available today, choosing the subset of content for your employees can feel daunting.

A/B testing is a tool used by marketeers to determine which advertising campaign will generate the best response. By setting up two similar but slightly different campaigns, you can determine how your employees engage with each campaign. Analyzing the results will help you determine which campaign to run more broadly.

You can set up A/B testing by choosing two target groups of employees. Then simply distribute one campaign to one group variation (let's get creative and call that group A) and the second variation to the second group (yeah, we'll call that group B). For example, you want them to get a better understanding of password management tools. For group A, you choose a whiteboard animation-style video. For group B, you pick a live action video dramatizing how a cybercriminal can steal passwords from a browser. After running the test, you see that in your organization, the group who received campaign B had a 51 percent higher completion rate and rated the content 34 percent more favorably than the group who received campaign A. Based on your test, you choose to roll out the content used in campaign B to a wider set of employees or all employees.

You may do variations of the A/B testing. One variation is to use the same content with different target audiences. Group A could be sales-related roles, and group B could be developers. You may also choose the groups based on location: Group A could be Japan, group B USA, and so on.

A/B testing will help you ensure that your employees receive the best possible experience and that you are using your energy and resources wisely.

A/B testing will help you ensure that your employees receive the best possible experience and that you are using your energy and resources wisely. The result will be happier employees, reduced risk, and better security.

Combining Metrics

The power of measuring really shines when comparing and combining different metrics. Using different measurements lets you examine different perspectives of your security

(continued)

(continued)

culture. Each perspective will give you new insights. You can also use the different perspectives to give meaning to other perspectives.

Let's use the example of phishing assessments. Your numbers show that 15 percent of your employees click phishing assessments. You also see that 15 percent of your employees are not completing their security awareness training programs. Most people would look at those two numbers and assume a connection. But is there really? Without digging deeper into the two numbers, you cannot know. Correlation does not equal causation. In this case it makes sense to look at each stat and see if the 15 percent of employees within each group are the same 15 percent each time. It also makes sense to look at the intersection between the two groups to see if they are the same. They might be, but just as likely they are completely different. The only way to know is to use multiple metrics.

Multiple Metrics, Single Score

You can also combine several metrics and represent them as a single score. You see this all the time. A good real-world example is something like the FICO score used to represent an individual's credit risk or worthiness. This is a single score, ranging from 300 to 850, that aggregates scores across several dimensions (for example, payment history, length of credit history, how much you owe, and so on); and each dimension has its own respective weighting.

This type of approach can also be used to represent the overall strength of a security culture. For example, the Security Culture Survey measures security culture across seven dimensions. Combining these dimensions into a single score allows for easy comparisons against other industries. That has value. Executives and boards of directors are always interested in knowing how their organization compares to similar organizations. This single score allows you to quickly reference the annual Security Culture Report and immediately know the answer.

You can combine any number of metrics into aggregated views and dashboards, providing you with a broader understanding of your current state. This type of dashboard view can be immensely helpful in giving you a quick reference of how you are doing and if there are any potential issues. It can also provide some great metrics that allow you to celebrate. Having all your important metrics in one simple, easy-to-read dashboard, and as trend data, will help you keep your finger on the pulse of your security culture management program. This can also be helpful when communicating with stakeholders and employees.

Trends

Trends can be a great way to track the progress and effectiveness of your security culture program. In Figure 9.1, we use *awareness*, as measured by employee knowledge (up is good), *behaviors*, as measured by phish-prone-percentage (down is good), and *culture*, as measured by the Security Culture Survey (up is good). Trending your results over multiple years may produce a similar trend graph. A major benefit of a trend chart is that the story tells itself; as knowledge and culture increase, risky behaviors decrease.

> *A major benefit of a trend chart is that the story tells itself; as knowledge and culture increase, risky behaviors decrease.*

Consider also adding data points for your target states so that you can easily see your gaps and track your progress. Hopefully, you will see that the gap is reduced year over year. Adding goals as data points adds the benefit of seeing how goals change over time.

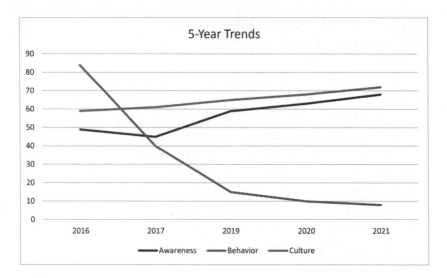

Figure 9.1   An example graph depicting trends for awareness, behavior, and culture

Our example was created very easily, using a spreadsheet and adding data points on an annual cadence. You may choose a different cadence based on your needs. You may also choose a different way to visualize your journey. The important thing is to find an effective way to easily track and communicate your progress, both for yourself and for your stakeholders.

Measure Iterations

Chapter 8, "Introducing the Security Culture Framework," discussed the need to measure each iteration of the process. The data you measure on each iteration should, at a minimum, be aligned with your goals and baseline measurements. When you get the hang of it, we recommend adding other useful metrics, such as:

- **Phish-prone percentage:** Do you notice large changes in the percentage of users who click simulated phishing tests from one iteration to the other?

- **Engagement with trainings:** Are there some training activities, content types, format types, or times of year that your people engage with more (or less) than others? Do some receive higher scores? Better completion rates?
- **Groups of employees:** Do some groups of employees stand out from the rest (positively or negatively)? Do some groups make larger or smaller improvements than others?
- **Manual data:** Did you perform observations, experimentations, or other manual measurements in this iteration? Add them as metrics.

A Note Regarding Completion Rates

People ask us all the time about completion rates and what they actually mean. What is the significance? Completion rates are one of those metrics that can be very useful if used correctly but are often misused and misunderstood. People tend to read more into completion rates than they should. They use completion rates as a measure of success—or lack of success. Instead, the best use case for a completion rate is to use it as a supporting metric—one that just might be able to help you to interpret your other measurements.

Imagine that you distribute a new training to all employees. You were expecting a large completion rate but were disappointed when only a small percentage of the employees completed the training. You wonder what is wrong. At this point, some may conclude that the employees do not care about security and start making elaborate plans to force employees to complete the trainings.

What if you jumped to conclusions here? What if you had other measurements you could use to guide you? Maybe you could have a look at your security culture score and notice that it's above the industry average and the data is showing that your employees have a higher-than-average knowledge of security. Then you might look and see that your employees are rarely failing phishing assessments.

Would you still come to the same conclusion—that your employees don't care about security? Probably not. Instead, you may start asking different questions. You might decide to check if there may have been a technical problem causing the training to not be delivered to the employees, or you might suddenly remember that a big portion of your employee population is out due to some event or holiday.

Completion rates can be a great source of information if used together with other data points, and as a supporting metric instead of as a primary indicator. It might indicate a problem, but this metric alone will rarely tell you the cause of the problem.

Takeaways

- Security culture is measurable.
- The most widely used and scientifically proven method for measuring security culture is currently the Security Culture Survey, created by Kai and his team.
- You already have access to systems and data that can be used to measure security culture even if you aren't able to gain access to the Security Culture Survey.
- Measure through observation, experimentation, surveys, and interviews.
- Consider using aggregated scoring, dashboards, and trends to visualize and communicate your status and progress.
- A single metric may not be sufficient to tell the full story. And data correlation doesn't equal causation. Expect to spend a bit of time analyzing your results to get to what the data reveals.

Chapter 10
How to Influence Culture

You get the culture you ignore.

John R. Childress

Culture is everywhere. Just as every organization has its own unique organizational culture, every organization also has its own unique *security* culture. And that means your organization already has a security culture, even if you don't yet have an established culture management program. It's up to you to make sure that your security culture reflects the knowledge, beliefs, values, and behaviors that properly represent the culture you desire.

This chapter explores how you can proactively influence your organization's security culture. Culture change can be both difficult and time consuming, but it doesn't have to be. By applying the right mixture of actions, at the right place and time, you can shape new ideas, shift behaviors, and improve perceptions of security.

Culture is constantly evolving and changing; it has an in-built plasticity.

Culture is constantly evolving and changing; it has an in-built plasticity.

This property of culture allows it to inform its members of what is accepted and what is not, as well as be informed by its members about the same. New ideas and behaviors can be introduced and adopted. Old ideas and behaviors can evolve or be discarded. Shaping culture is a constant and ongoing process where you'll always be evaluating (and reevaluating) the tactics needed to adapt to the current state and your target state. Another benefit of this property of culture is that you can target small parts of culture and improve it step by step, instead of being overwhelmed by trying to implement a multifaceted, global culture change initiative. Focus on the details, take one step at a time, and build your new culture. Small changes can have big payoffs.

Resistance to Change

At some point, you will undoubtedly meet resistance. The bigger the change, the stronger the resistance. This resistance is a normal human and societal reaction. So, when working to shape culture, you also need to plan how you will react to, or even remove, resistance to change.

One type of resistance is born out of our natural human tendency to be lazy. We humans (all of us) are lazy. We are wired to find the easiest way to accomplish a task. And even when we try to resist our own laziness, our minds are constantly seeking shortcuts to help conserve energy (Kahneman, 2011). Armed with this knowledge, you should always seek to make whatever behavior you want employees to exhibit the easy choice as opposed to the hard choice. In the behavior design world, this is all about reducing the friction associated with the desired behavior, making that behavior as small as possible, or finding ways to increase motivation at the point of behavior.[1] And, if you can't make the desired behavior easier or smaller, you might be able to make the undesirable behavior more difficult to achieve so that your target behavior becomes the easier option by comparison.

How can you achieve this? By working with human nature rather than against it. It will frequently be through technology, informed by the right kind of education, and supported by policies and social pressures. For example, if your employees are among the 50% of employees in Asia who use unauthorized file sharing services to get their job done, the answer is not stricter policies—they already know they are using tools that are not allowed. The better action is to understand *why* the employees feel the need to use tools that are not allowed. When you do understand the *why*, you can then help your employees by implementing better tools or processes. Select a file sharing tool that allows them to do their work and that your security and legal team have deemed acceptable from a risk perspective. Then help the employees transition into the new tool by making it super easy. Support the technology change by updating the policies and educating the employees and their managers on why this new tool is the best and how easy it is to use. Lastly, celebrate successes. Ensure that your people feel valued and seen for making the right choices.

Be Proactive

Culture is often neglected and ignored as a critical factor for managing security. Left in a corner, out of sight, culture is still growing, changing, influencing, and challenging the security of your organization.

---

[1] If you want to take a deep dive into behavior science, we recommend the work of BJ Fogg and Matt Wallaert as a starting place. You should also check out the behavior design chapter in Perry's book, *Transformational Security Awareness*, for specific applications of behavior design principles for security awareness. And, lastly, you'd benefit from listening to episode 3 of Perry's "8th Layer Insights" podcast where he interviews BJ Fogg, Matt Wallaert, and Alexandra Alhadeff: https://thecyberwire.com/podcasts/8th-layer-insights/3/notes.

Not all Resistance Is Resistance to Security

One caveat when dealing with resistance is that some of the noise generated by employees may be triggered by the change but may not actually be associated with the change. Some time ago, Kai's team was working with an organization in Oceania. Its 5,000 employees had responded to an assessment that allowed for open comments anonymously. The team got called in after an initial analysis by the customer. The customer was shocked and scared. They felt that their security program had failed because of several negative comments they received from employees.

After a call with the customer, the team performed a sentiment analysis of the comments, allowing them to categorize the comments into several groups. Kai's team quickly discovered that only a minority of the comments where about security, and those that were, were generally positive. Most of the negative comments were from employees taking the opportunity to vent anonymously about company issues completely unrelated to security. This led the customer to continue to expand their security culture program. They also stopped jumping to conclusions and instead leveraged their data and analytics to implement and improve their approaches.

Left in a corner, out of sight, culture is still growing, changing, influencing, and challenging the security of your organization.

Culture is present regardless of how it is dealt with. Ignorance is a choice. Over the past decade or so, we've seen many organizations experience disastrous outcomes because they tried to avoid the perceived complexity of managing their security culture. In that time, we also saw many organizations take control and improve their culture. The pattern is clear: Organizations that proactively engage in shaping their security culture demonstrate more resilience against threats; they involve the full workforce in defending the organization, and they bounce back much faster when faced with security incidents.

The Complexity of Culture

As we discussed in Chapter 6, the seven dimensions of security culture are interdependent. Influencing one dimensional element has a gravitational impact on the others. But, the interdependency of the seven dimensions is not equal across all of the dimensions. An important point is not only how they influence each other, but how their different combinations and strengths influence actual behavior.

Let's take an example in knowledge and attitudes. Knowledge, or *cognition*, as we describe it in the seven dimensions, is important. Knowledge has been shown to influence behavior on its own. However, in a clever comparison Roberts (2021) looked at how much the level of knowledge coincided with the levels of good behavior. He found a *correlation* between the two—demonstrating that as knowledge improves, so does behavior. However, when running the same comparison with *attitudes*, the outcome of the analysis showed that attitudes had a stronger correlation to behavior than knowledge alone. Knowledge and attitudes were also correlated.

This means that while knowledge improves behavior, it is most effective when changing attitudes, which themselves have a greater impact on behavior (see Figure 10.1). The idea of knowledge and attitudes being closely dependent and influencing each other is a theory that has been around for some time and is occasionally called the KAB model (knowledge, attitude, and behavior model (Khan et al., 2011). Other researchers and scientists also report similar results, either showing knowledge and attitudes are correlated or their joint influence over behavior (Pollini et al., 2021).

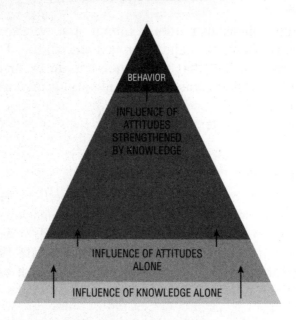

Figure 10.1 Knowledge and attitudes each can influence behavior. But attitudes strengthened by knowledge have the greatest impact.

Using the Seven Dimensions to Influence Your Security Culture

A security culture management program can target one or several of the dimensions to influence your organization's security culture. This section briefly examines each of the dimensions and offers suggestions for influencing that dimension. These suggestions are rooted in our experience from working with security culture. Along the way, we'll also incorporate interesting tips and findings from academic research.

Attitudes

Attitudes are a strong predictor of behavior. According to research conducted by Stephen Allen Roberts, PhD, in 2021, attitudes are a stronger predictor of behavior than knowledge alone. (That is not to say that knowledge does not matter—see the forthcoming "Cognition" section). Attitudes drive our acceptance of ideas and behaviors. By changing employees' attitudes toward security, the onboarding of ideas and the behavioral aspects of security can be directly influenced.

People Are Not Computers

Notice how we keep using the word *influence* when it comes to behavior change. That's because even with a good combination of attitudes and cognition, there is no guarantee that the desired behavior will follow. Anyone who has ever written out a list of New Year's resolutions can attest to the fact that there are plenty of times in life when we have all the requisite knowledge and the best of intentions, but we don't follow through on desired behaviors. Sometimes an overriding in-the-moment priority takes control. Sometimes habit and muscle memory (both literal and figurative) work against cognition and attitude. This is human nature, not an algebra problem. As we work to influence culture, we are working to increase the probability of achieving a desired behavioral outcome, not the certainty thereof.

Attitudes toward security can be influenced by explaining the *why*. Why is it important to the organization? Why should it be important for the employee? What are the positive and negative impacts associated with various security outcomes? Explaining and demonstrating how the right behavior is crucial for security can be very effective.

When working with attitudes, it is also critical to understand the difference between using the stick versus the carrot for motivation and reinforcement. Fear mongering and scare tactics may result in short-term behavioral compliance, but it has been shown that for long-term results, it is more effective to use intrinsic motivation. We propose a balanced approach, where policies are made clear and are enforced in those very rare cases someone is breaking the rules willfully. The rest of the time it is important to make examples of positive behaviors. For example, if an employee reports a security incident, even if it was their own behavior that caused the incident, the fact that they did report it should be celebrated. Use these kinds of stories to share the values and behaviors you would like to see. A key to building long-term habits is by making people feel incredibly successful (Fogg, 2020). Employees respond well to recognition, reward, and positive relational interactions.

Behaviors

Behaviors can be influenced both directly and indirectly. The most effective approach to changing behaviors is, and is likely to always be, to make it easy to do the right thing and difficult to do the wrong thing.

> *The most effective approach to changing behaviors is, and is likely to always be, to make it easy to do the right thing and difficult to do the wrong thing.*

In the book *Nudge* (Penguin Books, 2009), Thaler and Sunstein make a strong argument toward nudging employees (and others) to the right behaviors. Used deliberately to steer human actions toward a specific target, nudges should be considered in your security culture program, too. The strongest nudge possible is to make the action you want your employees to take the easiest or most obvious choice available.

For a more comprehensive understanding of behavior, you may consider the Fogg Behavior Model (`https://behaviormodel.org`), created by BJ Fogg PhD. This is a very easy-to-understand model that breaks behavior down into an equation:

$$B = MAP$$

Behavior equals *motivation* plus *ability* plus a *prompt* to do the behavior.

As described by Fogg, *behavior* happens when three things (motivation, ability, and prompt) come together at the same time. With this model, it's important to understand that motivation and ability have a compensatory relationship, and that is captured by a threshold, or what Fogg calls the "action line." If the behavior is hard to do, then the person will need more motivation to cross the action line. The secret to crossing the action line is the combination of sufficient *motivation* and a behavior that is achievable (*ability*) at the time of the *prompt*.[2]

Our primary culture research shows that at least 20% of employees worldwide report that shadow IT is common in their organization. What would happen if organizations had great approved tools, made them extremely easy to use, and promoted and celebrated their use? We'd likely see a dramatic drop in shadow IT.

Because behaviors are more influenced by attitudes than knowledge, information-oriented training alone will never be the most effective method of behavior change. This does not mean that training is not valuable, but it does suggest that your security culture management program needs to incorporate more than information-based training.

There is also a social component that influences behavior. As BJ Fogg says (see Figure 10.2), we must grapple with three truths about human nature: "We are lazy, social, and creatures of habit" (@bjfogg, 2011). We need to account for those realities in how we set our expectations and build our programs. We briefly touched on the aspects of laziness and habit earlier, but we cannot underestimate the power of social pressures and modeling.

Our behaviors are strongly influenced by group dynamics. We easily begin to mirror and internalize the behaviors and norms that we believe are acceptable and valued by the group.

---

[2]For more on this, see BJ Fogg's work, Perry's book *Transformational Security Awareness*, or episode 3 of Perry's "8th Layer Insights" podcast (https://thecyberwire.com/podcasts/8th-layer-insights/3/notes).

Figure 10.2   Three truths about human nature.

We easily begin to mirror and internalize the behaviors and norms that we believe are acceptable and valued by the group.

A powerful tactic to manage culture and behaviors is to continuously find ways to communicate behavioral expectations as being "just the way things are done here." And then remember to reinforce, reward, and celebrate.

Cognition

This dimension is about knowledge—how employees receive knowledge, interpret it, and apply it. As previously discussed, knowledge can influence behaviors and attitudes. You can use knowledge to train employees about correct procedures, help them discover threats, report suspicious behaviors, and more.

It is important to recognize the limitations of information-centric security awareness training. Knowledge (on its own) doesn't always translate to beliefs and values. There is very little academic support that security awareness training by itself will positively improve behaviors. (For an example, see the academic paper "Death by a Thousand Facts: Criticising the Technocratic Approach to Information Security Awareness," by Stewart & Lacey [2012]). Instead, research suggests that using training in combination with other means is more effective. For example, giving employees training that helps them to understand the broader scope of security (the *why*) is linked to their attitudes toward security, which in turn is a strong predictor of behaviors (as shown by the previously mentioned 2021 studies by Roberts and by Pollini, et al.).

A highly effective strategy that influences the cognition dimension is what can be considered "just-in-time" training or "teachable moments." If an employee fails a particular behavior, for example a phishing assessment, enrolling the employee in training that targets that specific behavior is very effective. An employee who fails one type of phishing assessment but not others is likely to change their behavior by learning to identify the key tells in that kind of phishing email.

A Quick Warning

Note here that by "just-in-time" and "teachable moments," we aren't necessarily advocating for immediately telling the employee that they failed. There is value in that approach only in that it provides the employee with immediate feedback; however, there is growing evidence that immediate training given at the time of a behavioral failure is not likely to be retained. The employee is emotional. They may feel entrapped or called out.

The importance of "just-in-time" training is that you've noticed a behavioral gap that needs to be addressed. You can do that by automatically assigning training to fill that gap that can be completed within a certain time frame. At all times, you need to focus on your relationship with the employee. Do everything you can to celebrate wins immediately and foster a strong relationship.

Cognition is about more than knowledge acquisition; it's also about the application of that knowledge. Knowing something and using that knowledge are not necessarily the same thing. When educating employees, it is vital that the knowledge itself is put to work. Support training with examples of good behaviors and what is considered "normal" in the organization, which has been shown to be especially effective when done by managers (see Uchendu et al., 2021). Use behavior management principles (mentioned previously), technology, and process to make it as easy as possible to do the right thing. Security knowledge alone is useless if it can't be applied in ways that reduce risk in your organization.

Communication

This dimension is about how the organization communicates regarding security-related topics. There is value in making security an ongoing talking point by employees all throughout the organization. Fostering a culture where employees feel safe to discuss security, both positively and negatively, will help normalize security as a concept and a responsibility. Self-efficacy is closely related to people's ability to learn and adapt to new security policies, as shown in an experiment by Hameed & Arachchilage (2021). Emotional safety is also important and has been shown to create a stronger and more resilient culture.

Culture varies greatly depending on geography. These differences include several factors—for example:

- How do we treat authority? (Will subordinates follow orders or challenge them if they disagree?)
- How rigid do we consider an organizational hierarchy to be? (Are you allowed to speak to your boss's boss, and what are considered acceptable topics to discuss?)

One of the top authorities on this topic is Erin Meyer, who, with her concept of the Culture Map (Meyer, 2016), has helped organizations and their employees to sort out a multitude of cross-cultural communication challenges. Her techniques should be considered for inclusion in your security culture program, especially if your organization is multinational or employs different nationalities.

Meyer makes the case that cultural differences exist on a continuum and that our own placement on the continuum is key to understanding how we differ from others. For example, we (Kai and Perry) are both from Western countries. That puts us on the opposite side of the cultural continuum compared to Eastern countries, like Japan. However, even though we are both from Western countries, we experience vast cultural differences from each other. Perry lives in the United States, and Kai lives in Norway—each country with its distinct cultural profiles and communication perspectives. These differences are reflected in how we communicate, how we perceive the world, what we value, and much more.

Failing to adapt communication to the cultural nuances of employees within a specific region could result in costly security mistakes. These mistakes are avoidable. Start by ensuring that all employees can learn in their preferred language. This isn't just about translating content; it's also about adapting that content to the local concepts and cultural context.

Another important part of communication is to listen to the organization. Do not limit yourself to monitoring incident reports and phishing assessments; make it easy for employees to discuss and report security-related topics. You may even implement culture carriers (often referred to as *security champions* or *security ambassadors*). These are employees in various departments, divisions, and regions of the organization who are given the opportunity to facilitate security conversations both from and to the security team. They are often a great way to make security accessible and give you additional ears on the ground. A nice bonus is that the culture carriers are usually normal employees who volunteer, using their intrinsic motivation to help their peers improve.

Compliance

The compliance dimension leverages policies and regulation to inform employees about expected security behaviors. As important as policies are, we cannot stress enough that policies need to be relatable to the employee, not only the policy maker. This can be difficult to achieve; legal requirements often mean that policies are written in a particular way. One suggestion is to make policies available in two parts: one part that has all the legal jargon, and a second part that explains the policy in everyday language. We have seen great success with this approach.

A policy needs to be well enforced. An unenforced policy communicates to your employees that they do not need to care about the rules. Your employees will take away the message that policies are there just for the sake of showing some legal or regulatory authority that they exist. Our suggestion is to use policies to document which behaviors and technologies are acceptable (and which are not). Breach of policy needs to have clear consequences, which in turn should depend on the nature of the policy and the breach. For example, some policies may require a mandatory training (failing a phishing assessment), whereas other policy violations may lead to termination (repeatedly sharing confidential information with an outsider). Policies are about clearly stating your standards of behavior, managing risk, and clearly communicating any potential consequences associated with failure to comply with the policy. Stating the repercussions in the policies is vital, as it gives your organization the right to enforce the policies.

Policy enforcement is key. If policies are not enforced consistently, employees are less likely to take them seriously. And if your policies are not enforced consistently up and down the organizational hierarchy, then you'll also have problems. This type of inconsistency leads to fractured trust and an unproductive relationship between the security team and the rest of the organization.

A Note About Policy Enforcement and Relationship Management

Although we make it a point that you must be able and willing to enforce policies, we also believe that you should write your policies and enforcement clauses in a way intended to foster positive relationships. Positive reinforcement, where possible, is best. Set good examples, share stories about employees doing the right things, and make it clear that security is a shared responsibility—policy or no policy.

Norms

Norms are the internal, unwritten rules of a group and its members. They are the unique social pressures and social structures that exist in all cultures and subcultures. They represent *the way things are done around here*. Norms can be expected beliefs, values, behaviors, use of language, and more.

Changing an organization's norms or a subgroup's norms is not as easy as changing policies and hoping for the best. Policies are important for helping to set expectations and guidelines, but you need to translate those policies into values and behaviors. Norms are strongly connected to a group's behavior. We've seen this at KnowBe4 Research as we examine phishing trends. The way groups act (their resilience or lack thereof) and react to phishing threats (such as reporting) reflects adherence to group norms. This means that norms are constantly influencing behaviors, but it also means that behaviors are constantly influencing norms. It's a two-way street.

This means that norms are constantly influencing behaviors, but it also means that behaviors are constantly influencing norms. It's a two-way street.

You can use behaviors to strengthen norms by communicating the types of behaviors that are acceptable and expected. Storytelling is a powerful way to embed norms. That's why our childhoods are filled with fables and morality tales. Society uses stories as a safe space to communicate expected norms, talk about existential threats, and to embed value systems within our minds. We can (and should) do the same in a security context.

When you observe a behavior that you would like to see more of, turn it into stories that you can share in your organization.[3] Talk

---

[3] If you are interested in learning how to craft great stories within a corporate leadership context, we recommend the book, *The Leader's Guide to Storytelling* by Steve Denning (Jossey-Bass, 2005). This is a great guide on how to create stories that helps transform norms and values.

about the behavior, what led to it, and what makes that behavior something to be celebrated. And don't forget to talk about what could happen if the behavior was missing. The behavior and your employees are the heroes of the story. That means you can also tell the story of what could have happened if your heroes didn't intervene. Telling the right story at the right time is directly connected to the result. Sharing stories in the right format allows other people throughout your organization to retell the story using their own words, while keeping the core message intact.

Your culture carriers (which we spoke of earlier) are also an important resource for embedding and reinforcing norms (Buss, 2017). Your culture carriers should be employees who already hold security in high regard. They have a good relationship with the security team, share core security values, and are able to communicate clearly the *why* behind many security decisions and policies. They live out security values and behaviors, serving as ambassadors in their day-to-day interactions.

Responsibilities

It is important for employees to *feel* that their decisions and behaviors have a direct impact on the organization's security. Shared responsibility holds communities together and makes people feel pride in their community. By feeling responsible, employees tap into an intrinsic motivation and are more likely to help their colleagues do the right thing. A feeling of responsibility gives employees the motivation to step up and act when no one else is; to contact the security team when they have questions; to propose better policies; to report suspicious behavior; and even to come forward when they know they've made a mistake. This sense of responsibility is a key to building human firewalls.

A feeling of responsibility gives employees the motivation to step up and act when no one else is; to contact the security team when they have questions; to propose better policies; to report suspicious behavior; and even to come forward when they know they've made a mistake. This sense of responsibility is a key to building human firewalls.

Most if not all organizations we have worked with have any number of employees who are not working with security but who are interested and curious. Curiosity and interest are often linked to a sense of belonging and a sense of responsibility toward their employer and their colleagues. This makes these individuals very valuable as *culture carriers.*

Recruiting and embedding culture carriers throughout your organization can be a very effective method to spread security culture. We do not mean hiring specific people to your security team; this is about recruiting volunteers—employees already working in the organization who are willing to take on volunteer tasks to spread information, set up lunch-and-learns, or just be reliable sources for security-related information or questions. Making these culture carriers visible, and giving them more in-depth training of security and its relevance to the workplace is likely to boost their motivation. Make them feel like they are part of an exclusive club. As a side benefit, you may even look within your pool of culture carriers as you recruit for open positions within the security team.

As with norms, storytelling and sharing examples of correct and expected behavior, where employees demonstrate that they took responsibility, can be very powerful. Focus on the positive aspects—for example, reporting a breach quickly, spotting a phish, challenging someone trying to enter without a badge, and so on. Make them feel like heroes.

How Do You Know Which Dimension to Target?

The seven dimensions of security culture are interdependent. Making a change to one often impacts the others. By placing intentional effort on influencing a single dimension, you should see measurable impact across multiple dimensions.

> *By placing intentional effort on influencing a single dimension, you should see measurable impact across multiple dimensions.*

The intricacies of the connections between the dimensions also mean that you could do something with one dimension that may have unintended negative consequences across other dimensions. But even that is valuable data. Strive to learn what happened and how the changes impacted the other dimensions. Avoid knee-jerk reactions to your findings. Be willing to experiment and refine your strategy over time.

We aren't suggesting a random approach to selecting which dimension(s) to focus on; rather, we suggest looking for low-hanging fruit. Using previous measurements, as discussed in Chapter 9, you should be able to identify areas that present themselves as easy (or obvious) targets. You can often find low-hanging fruit in multiple areas of your organization. Some teams, groups, or departments may stand out on one or several dimensions compared to the rest of the organization. Consider going after those. This is a pragmatic way to make progress and gain traction rather than getting stuck in analysis paralysis. You could also compare your organization to the industry-level benchmark: Are there areas and dimensions where you should improve?

You Are in It for the Long Haul

Remember that influencing your culture is an ongoing, long-term effort. You may have some quick wins, but steady improvement over long periods of time is the key to building a sustainable security culture.

Takeaways

- You get the culture you ignore. Your organization already has a security culture, even if you don't yet have an established culture management program.
- Culture is constantly evolving and changing; it has an in-built plasticity.
- Help employees understand the *why* behind policy, process, and technology decisions.
- The seven dimensions of security culture are interdependent; influencing one dimensional element often has a gravitational impact on the others.
- Everything is about fostering long-term relationships with your people.
- It is important for employees to feel that their decisions and behaviors have a direct impact on the organization's security. Shared responsibility holds communities together and makes people feel pride in their community.
- Steady improvement over long periods of time is the key to building a sustainable security culture.

Chapter 11
Culture Sticking Points

It is not our differences that divide us. It is our inability to recognize, accept, and celebrate those differences.

Audre Lorde

Each one of us is embedded in our own culture so completely that it is difficult to observe how our specific cultural influences impact the way we view everything around us. This cultural immersion is often so powerful that we are even blind to how our own culture constantly shifts and changes.

There is a common belief that changing culture is very difficult, but that couldn't be further from the truth. Culture is everchanging. The only constant in culture is change. That's good news. It means that an undesirable culture can be changed for the better. It's also challenging, however, in that it can be difficult to observe changes, and it is difficult to fully control the way a culture evolves.

This is true for any type of culture: from the culture of a country or region to the cultural mindsets and expressions of an age group, to the culture of an organization, department, or a subgroup of an organization. And sometimes we make missteps. Our immersion in our own culture creates biases and blind spots, allows for miscommunication and misinterpretation of motives, and can have the power to nullify an organization's otherwise well-intentioned and well-designed security program.

Our immersion in our own culture creates biases and blind spots, allows for miscommunication and misinterpretation of motives, and can have the power to nullify an organization's otherwise well-intentioned and well-designed security program.

If you are interested in influencing the security-related aspects of your larger organizational culture, then it's important to (as much as possible) find ways to remove the cultural biases and blind spots we all have. In this chapter, we'll explore a few of the tricky areas, gotchas, and challenges you can face when working with culture.

Does Culture Change Have to Be Difficult?

One thing almost everyone agrees on when it comes to culture is that culture is stubborn; it's hard to change. But that doesn't need to be the case. The idea that it is difficult to change culture is based on our inability to objectively view and interpret the culture we are a part of, including how it changes. Another reason for this idea comes down to there being a ton of anecdotal horror stories of failed organizational culture transformation programs around the world over the past 50 or so years. But here's the truth: Many of these failed initiatives come down to a lack of an adequate understanding of the organization's current culture, its future goals, and the purpose of the culture change program, as well as inadequate resources, a failure to handle resistance to change, and a general lack of cultural understanding and empathy.

Don't let the idea of culture change being difficult stop you from embarking on your journey of security culture transformation. That's a proven path to failure by simply not trying. Instead, let the tales of past difficulties be a source of motivation—to remove your blinders, plan well, and execute well. Implement the process from Chapter 8, "Introducing the Security Culture Framework," for a proven method for managing your organization's cultural change program. The one thing we can guarantee is that any culture transformation program will fail if you never initiate it. If you never begin, your culture will continually drift and be forever beyond your influence.

Using Norms Is a Double-Edged Sword

Humans are inherently social. We were born to be social. All our actions and activities are centered around being part of a group of other people.

> *Humans are inherently social. We were born to be social. All our actions and activities are centered around being part of a group of other people.*

Culture can be thought of as the manifestation of the fact that we are social creatures. There are many mechanisms inherent to humanity that need to be considered when working with security culture. One such mechanism is how we adjust to norms—those written and unwritten rules of behaviors. In a 2022 paper, Gregor Petrič and I (Kai) show that organizational norms are strongly related to the security-related behaviors of employees (Petrič & Roer, 2022). This paper explores both formal and informal norms, and how they influence susceptibility to phishing. We found that formal norms, like organizational policies and procedures, are stronger predictors of phishing behavior than personal norms. This is a clear indicator that organizational policies, as well as regulatory controls, are important; when implemented and communicated well, they make a notable difference (Petrič & Roer, 2022). Making sure that policies are up-to-date, reflective of the desired behavior, and communicated effectively should be considered a critical building block upon which the rest of your security program is founded.

Our peer-reviewed research also uncovered something surprising. The so-called *descriptive norms*—norms that describe the normal behaviors of a population—can be a valuable tool when applied correctly. The challenge is that if you are too enthusiastic about this approach and promote a new set of norms by sharing what is "normal" through examples, and the "normal" you are portraying is not the actual lived-out, observable behavioral norm within your organization, your employees notice the disconnect. When this happens, there is a huge risk that the employee population will decide to not follow your proposed "normal." And it gets worse: Our research found that employees may actually *worsen* their current security behaviors, directly impacting the security in a negative way (Petrič & Roer, 2022). Therefore, it's critical that you *walk the talk*.

Evangelizing norms can be very effective, but it must be done with care.

Failing to Plan Is Planning to Fail

Ad-hoc approaches are no longer adequate when it comes to the discipline of cybersecurity. (Yes, we use the word *discipline* very intentionally.) If you want to be able to proactively influence and predict where your security culture is evolving, then it is important to plan well, communicate broadly, and execute the plan diligently. Perhaps the most important factor of planning, however, is to plan for the unknown.

We have seen multiple security culture initiatives not meet their expected goals because the plan did not match reality. The same is true when an organization fails to adapt and change when needed: As your culture improves, so does your baseline status quo, which means that you'll need to adjust your future goals, targets, and metrics. Failure to embrace a continuous improvement model and mindset only leads to frustration. Culture drifts. If you aren't continually striving to adapt and move forward, you are falling behind.

Failure to embrace a continuous improvement model and mindset only leads to frustration. Culture drifts. If you aren't continually striving to adapt and move forward, you are falling behind.

And you can't afford to lose ground when it comes to cybersecurity.

If You Try to Work Against Human Nature, You Will Fail

Remember the second point from Perry's three realities of security awareness: "If you try to work *against* human nature, you will *fail*." We humans are lazy; that is a fact. We are wired to conserve energy and find the easiest, least effortful way to accomplish tasks. Armed with this knowledge, you can help your fellow colleagues by making it as easy as possible to do the right thing.

Here is an experiment for you: Choose a security control of your liking. Any control will do. Examine the control from the perspective of the end user and ask yourself: What other ways of doing this task exist? Make a list of the options, and then arrange them with the easiest option on the top and the most taxing on the bottom. Your security control should be on the top of the list, not toward the bottom. If it is not on the top, you have a job to do: You need to figure out how to make your security control the easy choice, the one action that employees are most likely to take in order to complete this task. Richard Thaler (2009) calls this the "default choice." Thaler's point is that, because humans are hard-wired to be lazy, we will always prefer to just go with the default option over having to decide how to do it, and then doing it.

The First Two Realities of Security Awareness

If you want to understand how the realities of security awareness are predictors of cultural sticking points, consider the following statements, implications, and resolutions:

Reality #1

- **Statement:** "Just because I'm *aware* doesn't mean that I *care*."
- **Implication:** Awareness doesn't lead to caring. And, if I don't care about something, I'm very unlikely to go out of my way to engage with it.
- **Resolution:** Connect security awareness messaging to topics, situations, and outcomes that your audience will naturally find relevant and meaningful. In cases where the connection is less intuitive, you need to help them "connect the dots." Don't neglect the power of emotion and story. The more human the ideas become, the better. Move away from abstract, security-centric information and connect the information to human-centric outcomes, purposes, and compelling visuals.

Reality #2

- **Statement:** "If you try to work *against* human nature, you will *fail*."
- **Implication:** Humans are wired in specific ways. We don't like to do things that are difficult, awkward, or require change.
- **Resolution:** When human nature makes performing secure behaviors difficult, you will need to either increase their motivation to perform the behavior (help

them remember or understand why it is important), or
you will need to find ways to make it easier for them
by helping to facilitate the correct behavior. This can
be accomplished with technology-based help or finding ways to prompt the correct behavior at the appropriate time. Even more difficult behaviors can begin to
become easy and intuitive when repeated enough times.
The goal is to create healthy security habits so that the
behavior no longer becomes an exercise in logic but
instead becomes engrained, effectively second nature.

Not Seeing the Culture You Are Embedded In

One of the most challenging aspects of culture is the fact that it
is very difficult for us to recognize our own cultures and cultural
artifacts. This leads to many problems when working with security
culture. One problem we see quite often is the security professional
who is so embedded in their own work that they fail to understand
that the other employees have other jobs, backgrounds, goals, and
so on. The security professional often becomes disgruntled, com-
plaining about how stupid their colleagues are. Instead, security
professionals should strive to understand why the other employees
behave as they do.

Similarly, a team of sales professionals may find it difficult to
understand why some of their non-sales colleagues behave the way
they do. We could go on, but you get the picture: We tend to see the
world through the eyes of the groups we are part of. Social media
has taken this bias to the next level by algorithmically filtering your
feed to show more of those things you care about, and less of everything else. The result becomes a narrow perspective of the world
and the choices we have, when in fact we have limitless options.

Breaking Away from Embedded Biases

To help you discover your own biases and limiting views, we suggest that you expose yourself to more cultures daily. Look at a foreign series or film on Netflix. Travel to a new country. Hire someone from a different location. Invite yourself to have coffee with colleagues from other departments or roles in your company. Whenever you discover something that seems amusing, challenging, or strange, as you surely will, ask yourself to what extent your own behaviors can be considered similarly by someone else.

Learning to question your own assumptions about awareness, behavior, and culture will make it much easier to build and maintain a good security culture.

Takeaways

- Our immersion in our own culture creates biases, blind spots, allows for miscommunication and misinterpretation of motives, and can have the power to nullify an organization's otherwise well-intentioned and well-designed security program.
- Policies and regulations are likely more effective than you think at driving security norms.
- Your employees will quickly discern if you believe and behave according to the norms you are evangelizing. If you fail to *walk the talk*, your employees' behaviors may get worse than before you tried to evangelize the norm.
- Failure to embrace a continuous improvement model and mindset only leads to frustration. Culture drifts. If you aren't continually striving to adapt and move forward, you are falling behind.
- If you try to work against human nature, you will fail. Seek to make the secure choice the easiest choice.

Chapter 12
Planning and Maturing Your Program

All you need is the plan, the road map, and the courage to press on to your destination.

Earl Nightingale

Now that you've had an overview of the moving parts, we'd like to offer some advice and perspective as you plan your program. You essentially have a bag of tools, the utility of which is entirely up to how you choose to use them. Improving your security culture takes time, effort, planning, and reflection.

The goal of this chapter is to remind you of some of the tools at your disposal, to highlight a few additional items that we've skimmed over until now, and to shed some light on the science of maturing your security culture.

Taking Stock of What We've Covered

We've come a long way so far! We've laid out the case for why security culture and the human defense layer needs to be a critical focus area of your security program and why it deserves attention at the highest levels of your organization. You've seen how traditional approaches to security awareness have failed because they didn't account for the *knowledge-intention-behavior gap* and the *three realities of security awareness*. We've worked to add precision to your understanding of what security culture is and what it looks like in both security contexts as well as from a traditional social sciences context.

With that groundwork complete, we added more precision by showing how security culture can be broken down into seven component parts, which we refer to as the *seven dimensions of security culture*:

- Attitudes
- Behaviors
- Cognition
- Communication
- Compliance
- Norms
- Responsibilities

From there, we discussed how you can use the Security Culture Framework to build your culture management program, how to measure security culture using the Security Culture Survey, and how you can begin proactively influencing your security culture via the seven dimensions. Along the way, we've warned you about some of the pitfalls and provided you with some insightful interviews from experts who specialize in culture.

Let's face it: That's a lot to absorb. We don't want to overwhelm you, but there are a few more tidbits we'd like to provide before we close out this book.

Know Your ABCs

As we mentioned previously, managing the human defense layer of your organization requires you to know your ABCs: awareness, behavior, and culture. For this book, we've been taking a high-level look at security culture management, which by necessity also includes awareness and behavior. However, we haven't done a deep dive into the science and tactics related to awareness or behavior. That's intentional.

Our focus for this book has been to expose you to the discipline of security culture as a social science as well as to provide you tools and frameworks needed to establish the programmatic and measurement aspects of a security culture management program. Although we mentioned the need for robust communication programs and that your program should include principles of behavior design where possible, we didn't discuss either of those areas in depth.

For an in-depth discussion of the communication science, behavior science, and culture-related tactics that you can use to support your security culture management program, we recommend Perry's previous book, *Transformational Security Awareness: What Neuroscientists, Storytellers, and Marketers Can Teach Us About Driving Secure Behaviors* (Wiley, 2019).

View Your Culture Through Your Employees' Eyes

Perspective is important. There's a famous quote (that tends to be attributed to a few different people): "There are three sides to every story: mine, yours, and the truth." Security culture is similar. There is the perception that you have about your culture; there is the perception that different individuals and groups may have about the culture; and then there is the perspective that you can get by zooming out—by aggregating everyone's thoughts and viewpoints—and which can be designed to cancel out biases.

This is the value of surveys. They help you take off the blinders and see the broader perspective. We highly recommend the use of surveys (such as our Security Culture Survey that we mentioned in Chapter 6) to help nullify assumptions and to gain an accurate understanding of your current state.

Also consider augmenting your survey results with data that can be pulled from various IT systems, such as your SIEM, DLP, employee-monitoring systems, help desk logs, and so on.

Culture Carriers

We'd also be remiss if we failed to reinforce the importance of building an internal network of security *culture carriers* within your organization (as mentioned in Chapter 10). These programs go by different names, such as *champion programs, advocate programs, security liaisons,* etc. The name doesn't matter as much as the function. We love the phrase *culture carrier*, however, because it truly signifies the significance of the function. This group of people carry and reflect the knowledge, beliefs, values, social norms, and behaviors that you want modeled.

> Your *culture carriers* are force multipliers for the messages and social norms you want reflected throughout the organization.

Building this group helps to ensure that there is a constant stream and reinforcement of security messaging moving through the organization. Consider your culture carriers as an extension of your team. They are your evangelists. They don't need to be security experts, but they should be influencers in their areas and have the ability to engage their peers in ways that are relevant and meaningful.

Building and Modeling Maturity

If you can remember all the way back to Chapter 3, you'll recall that we provided a quick overview of the Security Culture Maturity Model (SCMM) and promised to continue the discussion in this chapter.

Now that we've covered the necessary elements to create a program, we can take a deeper dive into the SCMM and discuss how it is unique. As we mentioned in Chapter 3, the SCMM (shown in Figure 12.1) is a new model that our team at KnowBe4 Research has been developing. The model is unique in that it is data-driven and evidence-based.

You'll notice that we mention our employer, KnowBe4, a few times in this section. That is due to the history of how we created the model and the datasets currently being used to inform the model. However, the Security Culture Maturity Model is for everyone. Our team at KnowBe4 Research is working to create tools that will allow anyone to leverage

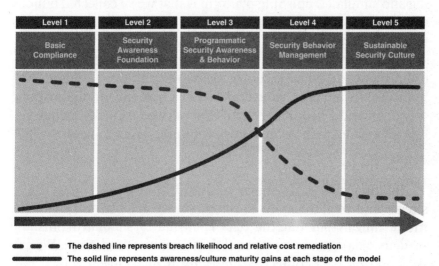

The dashed line represents breach likelihood and relative cost remediation
The solid line represents awareness/culture maturity gains at each stage of the model

Figure 12.1   The Security Culture Maturity Model (SCMM)

the SCMM regardless of if they are a KnowBe4 customer. The main advantage that KnowBe4 customers will have when using this model is that they will be able to leverage their dataset within the platform and likely have access to a richer dataset for analysis, benchmarking, and comparisons. You can keep up with our progress in this area by visiting the companion website for this book: https:// SecurityCultureBook.com.

Exploring the Data

One of KnowBe4's core missions is to provide customers with forward-thinking tools and resources to better understand their workforce's current risks and strengths. For example, the KnowBe4 platform provides reporting that allows customers to view their organizations' phish-prone percentage, understand industry benchmarks, view risk scores, survey employees, and more. And one side effect of being the world's most popular security awareness training and simulated phishing platform is that we've collected billions of data points from training campaigns, phishing simulations, and employee surveys.

All of this adds up, and, as a result, we have the largest dataset in the world when it comes to security culture. As Figure 12.2 indicates, we are now using that data in a new and groundbreaking way: to provide the industry's first data-driven maturity model specifically geared to measure security culture.

Culture Maturity Indicators

The dataset we have access to comprises several different elements. These range from training data elements to simulated phishing resilience data to organizational demographics, and more. We call each of these data points *Culture Maturity Indicators (CMIs).*

Table 12.1 lists a few example CMIs across various categories.

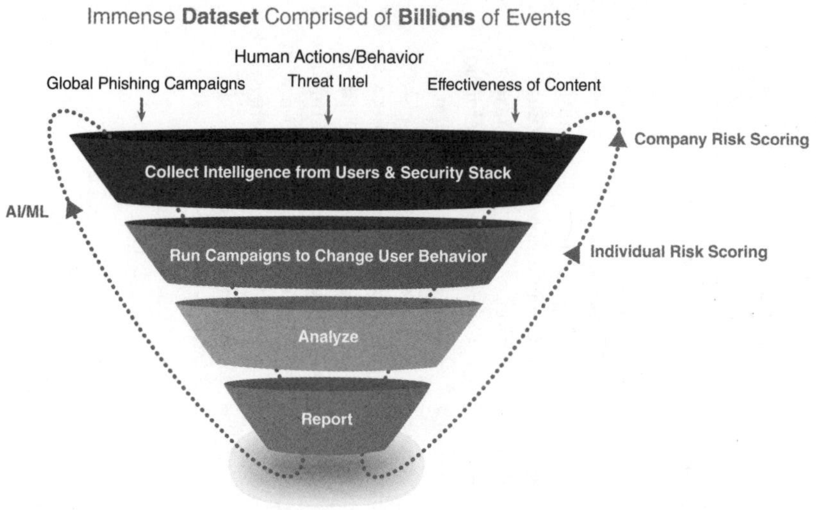

Immense **Dataset** Comprised of **Billions** of Events

Human Actions/Behavior

Global Phishing Campaigns   Threat Intel   Effectiveness of Content

Company Risk Scoring

Collect Intelligence from Users & Security Stack

AI/ML

Run Campaigns to Change User Behavior   Individual Risk Scoring

Analyze

Report

Figure 12.2   KnowBe4's immense dataset provides unique value to inform our model.

Each data point is useful on its own, albeit limited. The aggregation of several data points, however, can be used to paint a powerfully accurate picture of an organization's security culture—and that's where the SCMM comes in. With the SCMM, we are able to assign weights to each CMI, aggregate multiple CMIs, and derive the security culture maturity of a group based on the result.

The value here should not be underestimated. One CMI on its own is good but myopic. The aggregation of CMIs provides much needed perspective and accuracy.

> *One CMI on its own is good but myopic. The aggregation of CMIs provides much needed perspective and accuracy.*

For instance, an organization might be tempted to look at the SCMM and guess its position based on some of the activities it is currently engaged in, such as phishing simulations. But what if that organization is showing good results with phishing simulations, but their people don't understand some security concepts that are critically important

Table 12.1 Example Culture Maturity Indicators (CMIs) across various categories

Security Awareness Training	Phishing & Simulated Phishing Testing	Behavioral Data	Organizational Tone and Activities	Survey Data	Other Measurement Data
Frequency of training campaigns	Opened	Tracking & Reporting of simulated or real-world user behavior alerts	Company-wide communications regarding security policies	Culture Survey Data	Phish-prone percentage
Delivery types (in person, online, mobile, etc.)	Clicked	Documented policies for user behavior failures (stick) or high performance in testing/self-reporting (carrot)	Executive-led discussion around security policies	• Attitudes	Industry Benchmarks
Content types used	Attachment open	Technology/Integration into real-world behavior alerts	Presence/absence of Security Champions Program	• Behavior	Virtual Risk Officer information
Learning modules taken	Data entered on a landing page	Gamification	Reward and Contest regarding security behavior and culture including company-wide milestones, etc.	• Cognition	Email Exposure Check Data
Measured areas of strength or weakness	Exploited: user clicked on an Exploit enabled test		Security-centric special events	• Communication	API integration with other tools
Customization/personalization for the organization and their unique risks	Macro enabled: macro on an attachment was enabled.			• Compliance	
Customization/personalization for the individual based on role/department	Replied			• Norms	
	Reported			• Responsibility	
	Accuracy of reporting			Proficiency Assessment Data	
	Organizational patterns of use for phishing simulations (e.g., customization of templates, gamification, etc.)			• Passwords & Authentication	
				• Email security	
				• Internet use	
				• Social media	
				• Mobile devices	
				• Incident reporting	
				• Security Awareness	
				Others as desired	

in other areas? The SCMM accounts for this by factoring in multiple CMIs, each of which can be weighted and averaged before the model computes a final score and maturity level.

Let's briefly describe each level of the model, and then we'll show you some interesting ways it can be applied.

Level 1: Basic Compliance

Organizations at level 1 have usually been pushed into establishing a security awareness program by regulations and/or contractual obligations or because having such a program is seen as an industry best practice.

Organizations here do the bare minimum of training—for example, training based on policies/procedures mandated by a regulation or industry standard.

Metrics at this stage are usually focused on collecting the number of employees who have completed trainings, attended security meetings, etc. The program and metrics point to one goal: exposing employees to base-level mandated materials and providing proof that the employees have been exposed to the materials.

The organizational attitude at this level can be characterized as, "Let's just 'check the box' and move on."

Level 2: Security Awareness Foundation

Level 2 represents a significant departure from a compliance-driven program. Organizations here want to do more than the minimum. They understand the value in bringing awareness to threats, best practices, etc. They create resources or find ready-made resources to share as needed. This may also lead them to bring in vendors or create tools to serve their greater awareness needs.

Training is typically conducted during employee onboarding and annually thereafter; however, this level will also often include ad-hoc training, information sharing, or events based on perceived need or benefit.

As organizations mature, they may begin to increase the frequency of training or add more structure around how often they offer it. Similarly, as they progress through level 2, these organizations generally begin implementing more sophisticated methods for sending relevant information to different audiences and are doing so more frequently. They may begin working with internal marketing and PR departments, or they may begin adopting marketing-like practices on their own. These organizations don't stop with required training; they think about sending out information using multiple communication channels and doing more frequent trainings to keep security in the forefront.

More sophisticated organizations at this level will be considering practices such as segmentation of audiences, role- and risk-based message targeting, and continual messaging and training. They also generally use a diverse selection or content types and lengths that best match the diversity of the organization and the individual needs and preferences of the learner.

Organizations within level 2 may also begin conducting ad-hoc phishing simulations as part of an organizational security assessment; however, this is generally done only annually or quarterly and is not yet at a frequency to reliably reduce the organization's susceptibility to phishing.

Level 3: Programmatic Security Awareness & Behavior

At this level, organizations have tools in place. Their program has much greater structure than organizations at level 1 or 2. They are more intentional about how they choose content, who they send that content to, and the timing involved. Organizations here are also beginning their journey toward driving secure behaviors. They have tools in place for simulated phishing as well as having tools and processes in place for reporting suspected phishing events or other security incidents.

Organizations here are also beginning to focus not only on remediating undesirable behaviors (e.g., clicking on phishing links) but are also proactive about building positive security habits such as reporting suspected incidents, using a password manager, and more.

Over the past few years, many reports have made much of the fact that the vast majority of breaches are traced back to human error. This realization has served as motivation for many organizations to begin conducting frequent simulated phishing programs and encouraging the reporting of suspected phish. As such, most organizations we measure are currently at this level.

Training here is increasing in frequency. At the low end of maturity, organizations are testing and training quarterly. At the high end, they are usually doing some form of training at least monthly, if only for targeted groups.

As organizations climb the S-curve, they begin to see the real payoff: a measurable decline in risky behaviors. Additionally, this is where the likelihood of, and remediation costs associated with, breach begin to sharply decline.

Level 4: Security Behavior Management

Here's some great news: Phishing training is just the beginning. It represents only one category of how you can influence behavior to drive down risk. Approaching security awareness from a behavioral science perspective reveals several possible areas where behavioral interventions can be injected. As organizations pursue more advanced areas of behavior management, they begin to evaluate their policies, procedures, and technologies based on how compatible they are with human nature.

That's where level 4 comes in. Organizations at level 4 have made significant behavioral gains, and they are focusing on shifting multiple types of behaviors. They are also generally interested in understanding the "why" behind certain behaviors.

Organizations that approach security with a behavior mindset will have an eye to how their technologies, processes, and policies can begin to work with—or against—human nature to accomplish security goals. For instance, implementing a password manager is a great way to help people improve their password hygiene. And finding ways to reward desired security behaviors will help employees know when they are doing the right things and encourage them to do more of those types of behaviors.

Organizations at this level may begin collecting and evaluating behavior-related data across their security stack, their IT ecosystem, and more. They are looking at data provided from other security tools (e.g., SIEM, DLP, EPP, and others) to determine which behaviors need to be addressed. Behavioral interventions may have been defined for in-the-moment coaching, creating custom training campaigns and events that are as individual as possible.

At this point, metrics are generally being used to tell a story that is more nuanced than simply presenting data. Metrics and anecdotes are used to support the "human defense" and "human impact" that employees are having within the organization. And employees are being recognized as a critical defensive layer within the organization.

Training at this level could be categorized as continuous. This is all about in-the-moment coaching to remediate, reward, or reinforce behavioral outcomes.

Level 5: Sustainable Security Culture

Level 5 is the highest level of maturity. Organizations at this level intentionally and actively weave security-related values, beliefs, and behaviors into the cultural fabric of the organization. Specific attention is given to different contexts, use of social pressures, and the knowledge, values, and behaviors being reinforced.

Every organization has a security culture. An organization is only at level 5, however, when they are intentionally measuring, shaping, and reinforcing culture.

Every organization has a security culture. An organization is only at level 5, however, when they are intentionally measuring, shaping, and reinforcing culture.

This will have elements of compliance, general security awareness and communication methods, as well as behavior management, but all focused toward a larger goal: shaping the organization's unwritten values, norms, expectations, social pressures, and modeled behaviors.

Organizations at this level are working to embed security values throughout the organization and find ways to make their efforts sustainable for the long-term. Evidence of this includes robust behavioral intervention programs, establishment of reward and reinforcement programs, mature *culture carrier* programs, programs that leverage social pressures, reinforcement, continual messaging, and more.

Security values are woven through the fabric of the organization from the top down. Values are lived out and modeled by established employees so they are seen and can be "caught" by new employees. Security wins (e.g., reporting of phishing or other suspicious events) are celebrated. Security issues are viewed as an opportunity to better inform the organization through the use of stories and anecdotes. Security is viewed as a responsibility and a competitive advantage, not a chore.

Training frequency could be characterized as continuous training with a continuous improvement model associated with the program itself.

There Are Stories in the Data

When we decided to create the SCMM, the first thing we did was ask ourselves: What can we learn from the data we have?

> *When we decided to create the SCMM, the first thing we did was ask ourselves: What can we learn from the data we have?*

We wanted a maturity model that was based on the real world. We then ventured into the data to discover that there are distinct patterns of behavior, knowledge, and culture that, when put into perspective, tell a very compelling story. Have a look at Figure 12.3.

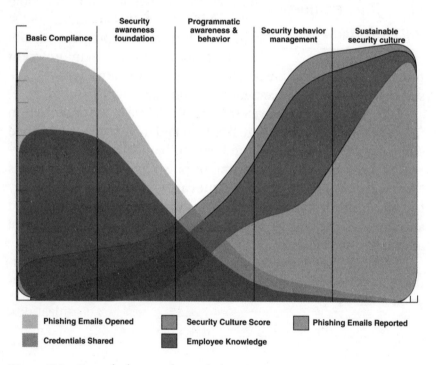

Figure 12.3   Example data overlay with the SCMM

This is one representation of a few CMIs plotted within the model. In this case, the CMIs we've plotted are five specific indicators:

- Simulated phishing emails opened
- Credentials shared as part of a simulated phishing campaign
- Security Culture Survey score
- Employee knowledge as reported by our Security Awareness Proficiency Assessment
- Phishing emails reported via the phish alert button

As you move from left to right through the five levels, maturity increases. The overlays represent data from each CMI. The two slopes that fall toward the middle of the model are behaviors you do not want to see—in this example, employees opening phishing emails and sharing of credentials. The three slopes that move up and to the right represent data from assessments on culture and awareness, and finally a behavior you want to see: employees reporting phishing emails.

This is exactly what you would expect to see as an organization becomes more mature: Bad behaviors are reduced, and good behaviors increase. Our data confirms that this is happening. Why is this important? First, because it shows that the SCMM is evidence-based; it is a simplified reflection of the real world. Second, by using data as part of the maturity model, we remove much of the guesswork that is involved with most maturity models. With the SCMM, you feed in your data and see where you are. Knowing where you are makes it easier to see what changes are needed for improvement.

Figure 12.4 shows another prototype data overlay.

This example aggregates two CMIs, KnowBe4's Security Awareness Proficiency Assessment (SAPA) and the Security Culture Survey (SCS) scores, across a large number of customer organizations. The two CMIs are aggregated to determine an organizational maturity score, and each organization is represented as one dot within a

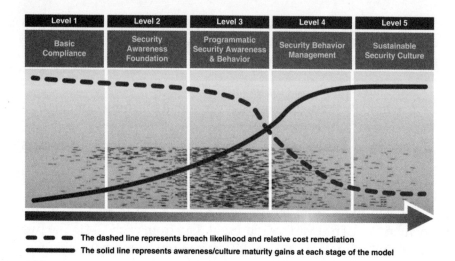

Level 1	Level 2	Level 3	Level 4	Level 5
Basic Compliance	Security Awareness Foundation	Programmatic Security Awareness & Behavior	Security Behavior Management	Sustainable Security Culture

━ ━ ━ The dashed line represents breach likelihood and relative cost remediation
━━━━ The solid line represents awareness/culture maturity gains at each stage of the model

Figure 12.4 Example of the SCMM showing maturity across organizational scores with KnowBe4's Security Awareness Proficiency Assessment and Security Culture Assessment as CMIs

scatter plot across the model. The example is useful in understanding the current maturity distribution of more than 40,000 organizations worldwide. Each of these CMIs on their own would have limited directional accuracy; when combined, however, they serve to add precision. When you look at the distribution of 40,000+ organizations across the model, you begin to see a story. You can see what the current state of the industry is and where the outliers are. If you know your specific organization's maturity level, you know if you are in line with the industry, falling behind, or leading the pack.

This is a prototype result based on real data, presented for illustrative purposes. In future research, more CMIs will be added to these models. Doing so will impact the distribution.

Here's another illustrative prototype (see Figure 12.5). Whereas the last example was across several thousand organizations, this example focuses on a single organization and shows how multiple CMIs provide context. This example shows an organization whose information sharing program is really only focused on doing the minimum, but they also engage in monthly phishing simulations and have been making good progress. Additionally, they sent out an awareness survey that returned its own assessment of their maturity, and they have some security technologies reporting observed behaviors. The CMIs used in this representation are as follows:

- **Basic awareness program:** If this were the only input, this organization would be at level 2.
- **Security survey score:** The results of this organization's security awareness assessment (on its own) would lead a model to believe they were in level 3.
- **Phishing program structure and results:** Strong results would indicate level 4.
- **Other observed behaviors:** Bringing in other observed behaviors (e.g., password hygiene and document sharing) provided evidence that this organization is in level 3.

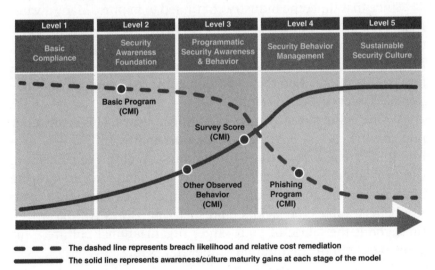

Figure 12.5 Example of the SCMM showing multiple CMIs of a single organization before arriving at the composite/average SCMM level.

Each CMI, on its own, provides only part of the picture. But, by looking at multiple CMIs, and because each CMI has an associated weighting, the model will much more accurately arrive at an organization's score and maturity level. In the example from Figure 12.5, the model would place the organization at level 3, *Programmatic Security Awareness & Behavior*, because that's the aggregated score achieved by evaluating the available CMIs.

A Seat at the Table

Building a robust program that follows a continuous improvement model and having the ability to plot your organization's maturity using evidence-based tools like the SCMM represents a step forward for the industry. Business executives, CEOs, and boards of directors are looking to the CISO to provide meaningful information. When the security-awareness industry introduced simulated phishing back in 2010, it was revolutionary. All of a sudden, security awareness leaders were able to demonstrate that they could measure and influence a key security behavior, and the need for this type of program was reinforced with the rise of ransomware.

Since that time, the industry continued to mature. Many awareness leaders evolved their programs to report relevant analytics pertaining to behavior change, human risk, and training engagement. These metrics were interesting to executive teams, boards, regulators, and auditors. And this evolution converged with the maturation of IT security as a discipline.

We are about to see the next evolutionary wave. This is the move into *security culture management* as a discipline. In this new evolution, awareness permeates throughout the entire organization. Cultural and behavioral norms become a driving force to mitigate human risk and to build up the human defense layer; and security beliefs, values, behaviors, and social pressures will be woven throughout the fabric of your larger organizational culture. This converges with the maturation of the CISO's role.

Takeaways

- Seek ways to view your culture through the eyes of your employees.
- Implement a culture carrier program to act as a force multiplier for the messages and social norms you want reflected throughout the organization.
- Aggregate multiple CMIs to provide greater perspective and accuracy.
- Visit the companion website for this book for more tools, updates, and resources for charting your security culture journey (`https://SecurityCultureBook`).
- We are about to see the next evolutionary wave: the move into security culture management as a discipline. This converges with the maturation of the CISO's role.

Chapter 13

Quick Tips for Gaining and Maintaining Support

A lot of times, people don't know what they want until you show it to them.

Steve Jobs

Let's say you've read everything in this book so far, and you feel ready to kick off your security culture program. You understand the moving parts around taking measurements and setting goals, and you have a good idea of the awareness, behavior management, and culture program elements that will be helpful and appropriate for your organization. All that is great, but there is still one critical component missing: buy-in.

For many reasons, gaining and maintaining executive buy-in is often seen as something of a dark art. This is because there is no standard formula that works every time across all organizations. Gaining buy-in is about connecting with other humans, each of whom have their own preferences and priorities, and convincing those humans that your program fits into what they believe is best for the organization and for them personally. In other words, you obtain buy-in by *selling*. Selling ideas and selling vision.

You Are a Guide

Let's start by acknowledging a sobering truth: Business leaders don't care about security for the sake of security alone.

> *Let's start by acknowledging a sobering truth: Business leaders don't care about security for the sake of security alone.*

What they care about is the result that a sound security strategy can provide and the impacts and risks associated with the lack of a sound security strategy. This is critical to understand. That truth should inform the methods you use to engage the organization, your executive team, and even the board of directors.

In these discussions, you need to have a personal guiding principle. Here it is:

Your Guiding Principle

Security is a journey and a conversation, *not* a destination and a directive.

Adopting this mindset is critical. It helps you approach C-suite and board conversations with the proper tone and expectations. By approaching security as a journey and making your security-related communication *journey-based*, you set the expectation that security doesn't just happen; instead, it's a continual journey—one in which you will almost certainly encounter detours, distractions, and even danger. And you are there to help guide the organization on this journey.

We are and never will be fully secure, hack proof, or breach proof. Rather, there are a series of progressive steps that we take in communication, conversation, and negotiation with the organization to help us navigate the security-related dangers, pitfalls, and villains associated with the *business* that we are in. Your journey, your story, is one of navigating these security-related perils as a way of managing risks to your organization's livelihood. This is all about business risk.

The journey/conversation mindset moves us out of the rigidity of binary decision-making and into a fluid and dynamic, risk-based conversation where your business leaders are primed to understand and appreciate the benefits associated with having a strong security culture.

Sell by Using Stories

As someone seeking to sell ideas, your first goal is to establish credibility and relevance. This comes through adopting the aforementioned guiding principle and by understanding the function and concerns of the people you need to obtain buy-in from.

As an example, let's say your goal is to gain buy-in from the board of directors. Your first step would be to understand the motivation and reasons for that group's existence, which is to help ensure the long-term health of the organization and to maximize shareholder value. So, your mission in showing relevance to the board is to demonstrate how security fits within that story.

Elevating your security conversation at a story level will also naturally guide you in deciding which metrics to share and what level of detail you should go into when discussing security-related projects, needs, trends, and concepts.

Always filter your conversation through the story.

Always filter your conversation through the story.

Be on the lookout for ways to:

- Align your program and elevator pitch to the organization's values, strategy, mission, and initiatives.
- Tie your program to known and understood compliance requirements.
- Use current events and stories about organizations similar to yours in terms of industry, size, or other demographic characteristics. (But avoid doing this in a way that could be perceived as alarmist or as fearmongering.)
- Map your program to established industry best practices (such as the NIST Cybersecurity Framework, the National Association of Corporate Directors guidance on cybersecurity, and so on).

The Power of Story

In the preceding section, we use the term "story" to reflect the framework of thinking and values through which your audience sees the world. That, of course, is just one type of story. You can—and should—become a storyteller. Always be on the lookout for analogies and anecdotes that help to make your points. There is a reason that oral histories were told as stories. And there is a reason that parents use morality tales to convey larger truths. It is because stories are the language of the mind.

Lead with Empathy, Know Your Audience

Research the stakeholders that you are seeking buy-in from to see what makes each of them tick. It's important that you know what their goals and values are within the organization. Be ready to sell them on the areas of your program that closely align with their values and goals. Show them that you are on their side and that your program will be helpful to them. You'll also need to address any specific concerns or pain points they may have.

Most of your "selling" and storytelling won't be in large, formal presentations; rather, they will be in less formal one-on-one discussions with individual stakeholders. That way, you can steadily build a system of support one person at a time. These people will then be ready to come to your aid if you later need to defend your program or position.

One tool that Perry's used for years to help prepare for these types of conversations is a brainstorming sheet for obtaining executive support. Figure 13.1 shows a generic example.

As you can see, the worksheet helps you pre-think through the finer points of how you'll craft the story (or business case) that you'll communicate with a specific individual. This is key. You won't have just one story; you'll have several flavors of your story, each crafted to capture the minds and address the concerns of individual stakeholders.

Figure 13.2 shows how the worksheet is used to capture the unique needs, motivations, concerns, and benefits that apply to each stakeholder. It's important to note that you aren't intended to share these worksheets with your stakeholders; the worksheets are used in your planning, to capture notes from conversations, and to craft the persuasive stories needed to obtain support.

Relationships are built on trust, and you can gain the trust of your stakeholders by truly seeking to understand them, making your conversations with them relevant, and continually demonstrating that you understand the business in a risk-centric manner rather than pushing your security agenda in an overbearing and binary manner.

Stakeholder Name	Title and Department	Stakeholder's Primary Business Drivers and Needs	Potential Stakeholder Concerns, Questions, etc.	Departmental Benefits If the Program Is Successful	Benefits to Stakeholder if the Program is Successful	Other Notes and Comments
Jane Doe	Head of ___	What is Jane's core business? How is Jane's success measured?	How might elements of your program feel like they work against Jane's core mission and values? Might elements of your program feel like they take focus from areas that Jane is measured against?	How might elements of your program make Jane's department look good? How might elements of your program help Jane's program perform better? How might elements of your program help Jane's department link to a greater organizational mission or support a broader goal?	How might elements of your program increase Jane's social currency? How might elements of your program help Jane's career? Can this help Jane feel connected with a greater cause?	Additional pre- or post-meeting thoughts go here.

Source: Transformational Security Awareness: What Neuroscientists, Storytellers, and Marketers Can Teach Us about Driving Secure Behaviors by Perry Carpenter

Figure 13.1 Example brainstorming worksheet for gaining support

Stakeholder Name	Title and Department	Stakeholder's Primary Business Drivers and Needs	Potential Stakeholder Concerns, Questions, etc.	Departmental Benefits if the Program Is Successful	Benefits to Stakeholder if the Program Is Successful	Other Notes and Comments
Mary H.	Head of Application Development	Needs developers to create solid code. On budget. On time.	May fear that training initiatives will take focus and time away from production activities and timelines.	Application developers will be more aware of the ways that attackers find and exploit vulnerabilities. They will be more conscientious as they develop applications and peer review code. As a result, there may be fewer security-related issues flagged during the Q&A cycle. There will also be fewer issues found during vulnerability scans. Fewer exploitable bugs make it into production.	The stakeholder will ultimately run a department filled with security-conscious coders who are known for developing reliable, secure code. Coders also see the stakeholder as someone who is enabling them to learn new skills and enhance their careers.	During meetings with Mary, we noticed that she feels like this is the "right thing to do," but has a number of production timeline commitments. She wants to wait until Q3. Can we potentially help evangelize this training and the benefits to the CIO so that she feels greater executive support?
Aliana R.	EVP of Legal					
Mark J.	VP of Marketing					
Name	Title of Department					
Name	Title of Department					
Etc.						

Source: *Transformational Security Awareness: What Neuroscientists, Storytellers, and Marketers Can Teach Us About Driving Secure Behaviors by Perry Carpenter*

Figure 13.2   Example brainstorming worksheet for gaining support (continued)

Set Expectations

One of the main reasons programs lose support is because the program's leader somehow failed to properly set and manage expectations. This comes down to clear and frequent communication. When it comes to security, you need to be careful to never over-promise. Security is about managing large sets of uncertainties. You'll never have a hack-proof, breach-proof organization. And no matter how good your culture program is, your people will still be human. So, you are always managing technology that is imperfect and people who are human.

Your story—and your expectation setting—is about layered resilience. It's about strengthening your layered defense. It's about increasing your capabilities to predict, prevent, detect, and respond to cyberthreats so that you can reduce business risk. And (when we are talking about a security culture initiative), it's about increasing resilience and decreasing business risk by influencing the security-related knowledge, beliefs, values, social norms, and behaviors of your people.

None of this happens overnight. While you will notice incremental improvements within relatively short amounts of time, you need to set proper expectations. This is a long-term, ongoing program that is always being adjusted and adapted following a continuous improvement methodology.

Be ultra-clear about where you are (your baseline), anything you know about organizations similar to yours (for comparison), where you expect to be in 6–12 months, and what your ultimate goal state is. And always, always, always, quickly communicate when you aren't going to be able to meet a stated objective. Doing so demonstrates integrity and self-awareness and, when paired with an otherwise good track record, builds long-term credibility.

Use Metrics, But Only Where Helpful

Metrics are critical in demonstrating how your program is doing. However, an inappropriate use of metrics can be confusing and distracting. Here are a few things to keep in mind when it comes to reporting:

- Avoid the temptation to report certain data simply because you have it. Instead, sift through the data and reports you have and find the things that are the most relevant to your program and help tell your story.
- Never provide a number or statistic without providing context. Tell your audience why that statistic matters. Why is it important enough to show?
- Never provide a number or statistic without providing an interpretation. If you provide a number without explaining what it means, you are leaving it up to the reader to come to their own conclusion, and their interpretation may be confusing or incorrect.
- Don't assume that you should report only hard data and metrics. Use stories and anecdotes to add depth to your reporting and to help humanize the data.

Takeaways

- Security is a journey and a conversation, *not* a destination and a directive.
- Gaining buy-in is about connecting with other humans, each of whom have their own preferences and priorities.
- Sell by using stories.
- Know what your stakeholders value.
- Be proactive when setting expectations.
- Use metrics, but only where helpful.

Chapter 14
Interviews with Security Culture Thought Leaders

You do not write your life with words...You write it with actions. What you think is not important. It is only important what you *do*.

Patrick Ness, A Monster Calls

One of the things we love about the cybersecurity community is that there is an already thriving group of individuals who focus day in and day out on improving the security culture of their organization or the organizations they serve. There are individuals running programs that have moved far beyond mere security awareness and are approaching the human side of things in a transformational way. This chapter is a small glimpse into the collected wisdom and experience within our community. Sadly, we were not able interview all the people we admire, but we can bring you a representative sample.

The format of this chapter is simple, we sent a list of seven questions to several thought leaders and asked each of them to (as their time allowed) complete at least four of the questions. This allowed each expert to focus on the questions they were most passionate about.

We asked the following questions:
- Why is culture important?
- Why do you find culture interesting?
- Is there a specific definition of culture that you find useful?
- How do you use metrics to improve culture / measure the effectiveness of cultural change?
- What actions can be taken to direct cultural change?
- Is there a success or horror story you'd like to share related to culture change? (Alternative question: What is your most interesting experience with culture?)
- How does a culture evolve (or how often)?

If you had a sense of *déjà vu* as you were reading those questions, it's because these are the same questions we asked experts in Chapter 7. The reason for doing this is simple: so that we can observe interesting intersections or departures of thought between those culture experts who don't specialize in security and those who do. In the end, we see that culture is culture. The only significant difference is which aspects of culture someone focuses on.

Enjoy!

Alexandra Panaretos, Ernst & Young

- **Name:** Alexandra Panaretos
- **Title:** EY Americas Leader for Human Cyber Risk
- **Organization:** Ernst & Young, LLP

Why Is Culture Important?

Culture is a vital part of any organization or group because it offers a solid connection to the past and can provide a clear purpose and strategy for the future. The successful construction of any community requires language, education, and traditions that give the members a sense of belonging, an expectation of behavior, shared interests, and shared values. Culture ensures the survival of a community at the most primal level. Still, beyond that, it gives members motivation to contribute to the group's success.

Although culture within any group, community, or society is of great significance, it is also an essential element of how they are viewed from the outside. As an example, we can look at the United States military's long-standing culture of security and secure behaviors. For better or worse, our armed forces are viewed by the civilian community in certain ways due to, in large part, this long-standing culture. Among the different branches, there are a variety of cultural norms, and this even affects how the individual units view one another.

Culture in the workplace is no exception; a company's culture is sure to influence how it is perceived by clients, customers, and investors, and even how different departments or organizations within view one another. Without question, it is an essential aspect of a company's cybersecurity success. When the employees and public know a company's culture, they can ascertain its trustworthiness and ability to handle all the challenges of maintaining a secure organization.

Why Do You Find Culture Interesting?

Observing how culture defines and shapes a company or community is of great interest to me, particularly their cybersecurity culture. It is fascinating to observe how culture can create a space to either challenge traditional thought processes and enable fresh perspectives or cultivate a group-think philosophy that may hinder progress.

As our collective world and technologies change, shifts in cultural expectations are inevitable for any group, and a company's cybersecurity success may depend on managing and learning to cultivate these expectations within the company culture.

My children have provided excellent examples of adjusting to cultural norms and expectations in a digitally centered world. They have managed to adapt to various changes and challenges throughout these last few years by cultivating new ways to connect with their friends, teachers, and family. They continue to strengthen the culture amongst their peers to accommodate new technologies, changing expectations, societal standards, and the physical and emotional challenges they face as children growing up in the world today.

Observing how clients have adapted their security culture throughout the years has been fascinating to me, from how leadership has succeeded or failed to how the employees have adjusted to how customers and communities view those changes in culture. Learning how various organizations build secure cultures also inspires thoughtful consideration about the communities in which I belong. It is one of the many reasons I volunteer with youth and senior organizations to teach secure behaviors and address concerns found in both online and offline activities.

Is There a Success or Horror Story You'd Like to Share Related to Culture Change?

This is a success story.

I was once hired by a company that had experienced a substantial leadership change. The CISO knew their relationships with the business units would determine their future success.

One of my first observations of the organization members was how they seemed to go out of their way to avoid interacting with the security function. The training modules and the cookie-cutter awareness campaigns? Completely ineffective. A true compliance exercise at best.

This CISO had grown weary of a narrative that suggested people were foolish and that the "weakest link in the process" was responsible and challenged the security team to think differently. The frustration with the status quo was palpable.

They wanted to be a valued partner and advisor to the business units. But across all vendors, there was a standard recipe for training, phishing assessments, and campaign themes, none of which improved the cybersecurity risk profile of the organization.

The team and I discussed how most cybercrimes thrive in the disconnect between the digital realm and the physical working world. Phishing wasn't an innovative crime; it has existed since the days of the Wild West and the telegraph. Whether manipulating an individual occurred in a letter carried by the pony express or in an email, the crime was the same and indeed not a new concept.

However historic the crime may be, cybersecurity can seem like an imperceptible threat for most. How could we change the perception of security? What could we do to be intentionally different? How could we connect an intangible digital risk to real-world behavior?

In the days that followed, surrounded by colorful boards filled with the byproducts of extensive brainstorming sessions, two simple questions changed the trajectory of the human risk strategy.

What would happen if we told people to trust their instincts? Do people realize they know more than they think they do when it comes to cybersecurity?

It became one of the defining moments of my career in human risk mitigation. People didn't need to know everything. People needed to know *enough*—enough to recognize a threat, enough to feel confident in their actions when faced with a challenge, or enough to know they needed assistance.

One can quickly sense danger when confronted with flames and smoke, but how would you activate that same primal instinct in the digital world with no tangible association to a threat? In a world surrounded by constant noise, had we stopped paying attention to our intuition? How could we teach people to listen to that intuition and trust their gut when something didn't seem right in their digital or work activity?

We knew the success of the CISO's vision hinged on engagement with the workforce and enabling them with the confidence to seek out the security team with their questions or concerns. They had to trust us.

Inspired in part by too much caffeine and too little sleep, we created a campaign based on memes.

I'm serious. Not kidding at all.

No computer training modules. No emails people wouldn't read. We wanted people to stop, to have a surprising reaction to what they viewed on the digital signage. We knew we didn't want it to resemble anything else.

Culture change began with a sarcastic comment, brilliant marketing minds, and a joke.

The premise was simple: Use situations that anyone could imagine themselves in. Those moments we share across cultures, genders, and languages and tie them to security. Dare to be different. Rebrand security as human. Provide the opportunity for people to be amazed that it originated from the security team. Build trust through shared experiences and laughter.

And it worked.

The cybersecurity team generated memes, one of my favorites being "You know when something seems off," accompanied by a photo of a woman smelling a carton of milk, with the call to action simply, "Contact the Information Security team with questions" and the department's contact information. Another favorite was a photo of a child holding markers and lipstick in front of a wall of scribbles. "You know this isn't going to end well" was the tagline.

Every parent we knew reacted to that one. The collateral material that accompanied the meme launch provided actionable tips, "did you know" trivia, and links to relevant policies or procedures.

The feedback was incredible. Traffic to the intranet site grew exponentially, and the shared mailbox yielded trends and data points we didn't expect. We found the engagement we needed to embed security behaviors into every function of the enterprise and build the foundation of a secure culture.

In the months that followed, we solicited photos for the memes from employees, which turned into a contest. Individuals were recognized and rewarded for having the funniest meme of the month, while business functions competed against each other to take the top prize. The campaigns allowed us to build relationships organically and take every opportunity to be neighborly with the business. We leveraged the additional benefit of creating a self-generating content stream for the program in the process.

Security was able to partner with human resources and assist with helpful advice to protect one's identity during benefits enrollment. Teaming with the finance department, they created the opportunity to demonstrate how to use digital banking and online wallets safely during the holiday shopping season; with each interaction, security made sense. People began to understand how a single click could lead to data or financial loss. Employees were taught cyber hygiene with simple, point-in-time prompts, where individuals were most likely to encounter a threat or risk. One of our most successful efforts took place around the holidays, where the security team provided a guide to securing devices people were likely to give or receive as gifts.

Not long ago, I checked in with resources still on the team. While the meme contest has been retired, the lines of communication and the understanding of secure behaviors continue to thrive.

The team's ability to stand out above the corporate noise and a focus on building relationships formed a culture of security that permeated every aspect of the company and thrives today.

Dr. Jessica Barker, Cygenta

- **Name:** Dr. Jessica Barker
- **Title:** Co-CEO, Co-Founder, & Socio-Technical Lead
- **Organization:** Cygenta

Why Is Security Culture Important?

From a security perspective, culture is important because it is the foundation on which an organization's entire security posture rests. Security culture impacts everything from the extent to which people practice positive security behaviours to the way in which different teams interact with the security function (and vice versa) to whether people report security incidents when they occur. This last point is one of the most important, because if there is a culture of fear around security in an organization, people will often avoid reporting if they have clicked on a link in a suspicious email, for example. A culture of blame doesn't reduce the likelihood of further incidents; it just reduces the likelihood of the security team being aware of them. Sidney Dekker's work on just culture is fundamental here.

Why Do You Find Culture Interesting?

As someone with a background in sociology, I've always found culture fascinating: why we behave as we do, how we can be influenced, the stories we tell, and the symbols we choose to capture and represent meaning. Many people working in security grew up fascinated by how machines work; I grew up fascinated by what makes people tick.

What Actions Can Be Taken to Direct Cultural Change?

One of the most important factors in cultural change is the tone from the top—the extent to which leadership demonstrates that security is a cultural value for the organization. This is partly due to principles of social proof: If we don't know what to do, we mimic the behaviour of those around us, especially those in authority and those we relate to. This is also why cyber security champions programmes can be so effective. In a champions (or ambassadors) programme, security is not just being driven by the security function but also by a community of champions. These champions are not experts in security but the friendly voice and ears of security in different teams.

At Cygenta, we've seen huge inroads made with champions programmes we've helped organizations build, because they can break down barriers between security and the rest of the organization, facilitating two-way communications where the security function is able to listen to colleagues throughout the business much more effectively.

What Is Your Most Interesting Experience with Culture?

One of the most interesting experiences I've had with security culture was working with an organization where the same people were persistently practicing unsecure behaviours. For a long time, the organization tried to handle this with punitive measures: mandatory training (that was quite dull!), warning emails, warnings to individuals' line managers, and even threats of restricting their internet access. When they brought us in, there was talk of firing these individuals (who they referred to as "repeat offenders"). We worked with the organization to assess the cyber security culture and then develop a roadmap to a more positive and proactive security culture.

As part of this, we helped them build a cyber security champions programme in which the so-called "repeat offenders" were encouraged to become security champions. The overwhelming majority engaged really positively in the programme, and we saw a huge turnaround in their security practices. They helped the security team identify security friction and areas where people were consistently practicing security workarounds. The security team responded positively and improved policy, processes, communications, and tools. The so-called "repeat offenders" became security advocates leading change.

Kathryn Djebbar, Jaguar Land Rover

- **Name:** Kathryn Djebbar
- **Title:** Senior Cyber Security Education & Culture Specialist
- **Organization:** Jaguar Land Rover

Why Is Culture Important?

Culture is important from an evolutionary standpoint; it allows us to learn from others' mistakes and evolve into better ways of doing things. It also allows humankind a contextual background for understanding others and behaviours that are socially acceptable within a group setting, be that organizational, geographical, or interest-based.

Why Do You Find Culture Interesting?

I find culture fascinating due to the diversity it affords human nature. It is an innovative and constantly changing concept. As Walt Disney once said, "We keep moving forward, opening up new doors and doing new things, because we're curious...and curiosity keeps leading us down new paths."

I believe there are several different methods to achieve the same outcome, but due to the individualistic nature of humankind, one size does not fit all. Culture is a similar concept to the notion of intelligence in that regard. Someone who is 'book-smart' and academic is intelligent in a different way to that of a tribesman in the Amazon—if they were to switch roles at a moment's notice, they would find it very difficult to adjust to the others, way of life; however, both individuals are able to utilise their skills to survive and lead a fulfilling way of life.

Is There a Specific Definition of Culture That You Find Useful?

"Culture in its broadest sense is cultivated behavior; that is the totality of a person's learned, accumulated experience which is socially transmitted, or more briefly, behavior through social learning."

I find this a useful definition, as it pertains to the social experience of culture and learning through others.

How Do You Use Metrics to Improve Culture / Measure the Effectiveness of Cultural Change?

In an organizational setting, defining baseline measurements that support organizational outcomes is the most important step to determine whether change initiatives are working for or against the success of the business. Ultimately, most factors will boil down to financial outcomes; however, it is also important to consider reputational aspects, as an organization will always have a brand image they want to convey and a market segment they wish to appeal to.

In tandem with this, employee satisfaction is a key metric to define and measure, as people are at the heart of an organization, and without the right people, the business will struggle to achieve its desired outcomes. Therefore, employee satisfaction or "pulse" surveys, in addition to conducting focus group exercises, are a key method of measuring both quantitatively and qualitatively in order to develop a deeper understanding of what is going on in terms of the culture.

What Actions Can Be Taken to Direct Cultural Change?

I believe the two key components to achieving cultural change are communication and transparency. Yes, there are many different models and theories of change that have been developed over time; however, if you look closely at all of them, the main themes here are communication and transparency.

That means that the board are open and honest about the impact of certain factors on business goals and what that looks like for the future of the company. There also needs to be an element of openness with "shop-floor" staff who should be in a position to challenge and voice their concerns over change, which in turn needs to be heard and addressed appropriately.

If neither communication nor transparency is used, people will continue to do what they have always done, and those behaviours will continue to be passed down through generations at detriment to the organization.

Lauren Zink, Boeing

- **Name:** Lauren Zink
- **Title:** Sr. Security Awareness Specialist
- **Organization:** Boeing

Why Is Culture Important?

Culture is significant to any organization, whether it be their people culture, leadership culture, or, more specifically, the security culture. A culture of any kind can make or break an organization. In the people/leadership realm, it can help either retain good talent or cause you to lose it, whereas in the security realm it either can help you preserve your top customers or make them walk away, which, in turn can cause irrefutable reputational damage.

It is essential to clearly define the correct actions employees should take and train them on how to take them when it comes to security incidents. And patience is a virtue when it comes to truly creating a shift in culture, as it won't just happen overnight. It requires buy-in from the top down, and back up again. It is unique because shifting a culture can't just fall on the shoulders of one person or group; it is truly a team effort that involves everyone in the organization having a solid understanding of security risks as well as how to react to said risks when they are faced with them.

Once the behaviors are learned and understood, a next step to help ensure success in a culture is to start to reward those who demonstrate the correct behaviors. This successively helps security behaviors to become positive habits as well as allows people within your organization to feel empowered to be security-aware both at work and at home. When considering the build out of any security program, cyber hygiene and awareness should be a high priority in order to help guide and lead the security culture shift at all layers of the organization.

Why Do You Find Culture Interesting?

Culture is intriguing because it really is its own beast, and there are so many variables when it comes to creating a true shift and quantifying that change. It is never an easy task at an organization, but once you are able to demonstrate and measure that security cultural shift, it is so very rewarding and makes the heavy lift worth every painstaking moment you put into it. Security culture is also fascinating because it pulls in so many other elements outside of security, including, but not limited to, psychology, sociology, marketing, communications, and even learning and education. Outside of security awareness, there are not many other positions within security where one gets to bring together so many various aspects to help create a true change to better the security and safety of an organization and its people.

Is There a Specific Definition of Culture That You Find Useful?

Culture is when achievements are formed as a collective.

More specifically, security culture should be taught as creating a new habit or mindset that becomes so natural it in turn becomes engrained in a person's day-to-day routine. These positive security habits then play a larger role in protecting a company, its information, its assets and its people.

How Do You Use Metrics to Improve Culture / Measure the Effectiveness of Cultural Change?

Metrics and measurements that demonstrate cultural shift can sometimes be challenging to come by, especially if a program is still in its infancy stages. However, it is essential to try to capture as much information in these beginning stages as possible to then turn around and measure against to validate growth over time. Metrics that measure a behavioral change or a shift in baseline knowledge are an effective way to calculate an improvement in security culture.

One way to measure behavioral change is to look at the amount of human error-related incidents being reported to your company's help desk and/or SOC. Work with those teams to identify areas of concern or groups with high incident rates and conduct various awareness campaigns that align to these specific areas. In order to go a step further, target these awareness campaigns to specific groups that are creating these high numbers. As the awareness team conducts various campaigns, stats and metrics should be captured to measure if the human error-related incidents start to move in a varying direction.

An easier win in the area of measuring cultural change could be done in the form of a survey or focus groups. This allows measurement of baseline knowledge, as well as quantitative and qualitative feedback that can be garnered regarding security risks and an understanding of the company's security program. The same questions measured over and over again after awareness campaigns and training are deployed should demonstrate a shift in baseline knowledge and understanding.

A successful practice to employ is to share whatever metrics are chosen for measurement at your organization. Communicating this information allows for transparency, helping paint a bigger picture so employees can truly understand how they contribute to the overall positive shift of security and safety culture at the organization.

Mark Majewski, Rock Central

- **Name:** Mark Majewski
- **Title:** Information Security Evangelist
- **Organization:** Rock Central

Why Is Culture Important?

Without a culture change, awareness and behavior change will slip back to previous norms. Sustainable behavior change can only be successful when accompanied with sustainable culture change.

Why Do You Find Culture Interesting?

Culture is fascinating because there is no obvious and easy path to changing culture. Much like a garden, you can set it up for success, but it will ultimately be influenced by nature.

Is There a Specific Definition of Culture That You Find Useful?

A common definition of culture is "an organization's shared norms, values, and expectations." I also think that culture can be defined as "the residue of common behaviors within an organization."

How Do You Use Metrics to Improve Culture / Measure the Effectiveness of Cultural Change?

I conduct a periodic/annual culture survey. However, this survey does not ask questions like *how well can you identify a phishing email?* or *do you know how to make a strong password?* because these questions attempt to measure knowledge. Knowledge is important, but less important than behaviors. And I can test behaviors with things like simulations and observations. Instead, my culture surveys ask more about the organization's environment. Things like *is protecting client data a priority in your company?* or *do your peers actively protect sensitive data?*

What Actions Can Be Taken to Direct Cultural Change?

Some common ways to direct culture change in a positive direction are:

- Get senior leader buy-in.
- Align senior leader behaviors to match desired norms (lead by example).
- Include InfoSec as a visible priority in business goals, metrics, KPIs, OKRs, etc.
- When training or reinforcing secure behaviors, in addition to communicating what team members should know and the appropriate behaviors, include *why* it is important.
- Garner team member concern by describing the current threat landscape by referencing recent news reports. This helps reinforce that the threat is real.

Is There a Success or Horror Story You'd Like to Share Related to Culture Change?

I have seen the power of culture change. After attending the funeral of an employee who died during a work-related fatality, the CEO made safety the #1 priority. He never wanted to have to address the family of a fallen employee. As a company, we developed a safety culture change initiative, which included several years of emphasizing the importance of safety: in the statement of corporate goals, in daily pre-work huddles, in every meeting agenda, in every employee's performance review, and more.

After several years, the outcome of this laser focus on safety was that the company was ranked in a company benchmark survey as the #1 safety cultured organization in North America...by many points. In fact, the survey conductors were skeptical of the results, until they witnessed the culture themselves during their on-site visits. You could see safety messages and behaviors everywhere...even in the corporate offices. As an example, it was very common to see several employees (sometimes senior leaders) rushing to clean up a spill in a walkway and immediately mark it with a safety cone so that no one would slip. I learned that with the right level of focus and commitment, true company culture change was possible.

How Does a Culture Evolve (or How Often?)

Culture change is slow. It can take three or more years to really drive a meaningful culture change.

You know you are successful in a culture change initiative when team members are influenced not only by their leaders but also by the behaviors of their peers. Sustainable security culture change cannot be driven only by centralized security awareness and culture-change teams. It requires the engagement of team members across the organization as culture deputies.

Mo Amin, moamin.com

- **Name:** Mo Amin
- **Title:** Independent Consultant
- **Organization:** moamin.com

Why Is Culture Important?

It's important because at a fundamental level you need to appreciate who your fellow humans are, how they behave and interact in a given environment, to be able to affect positive change.

Why Do You Find Culture Interesting?

Fundamentally, it's actually a mix of people, technology, and the interaction between them. I find that interesting.

Is There a Specific Definition of Culture That You Find Useful?

No, I don't believe in attempting to define culture, as every organization is different and typically there are multiple and varying ways people work and behave. Although we live in a digital world, organizations are analogue; that is to say, they are continuously variable.

In my experience it's best to listen and watch how things are done, and soon you'll begin to appreciate the nuances. I look for how different personalities interact, the politics across different teams, and the trust relationships within the organization.

How Do You Use Metrics to Improve Culture / Measure the Effectiveness of Cultural Change?

In my experience, the most valuable piece of work one can do is to develop and run a security culture study or similar. A combination of surveys, focus groups, and one-to-one sessions where you seek to understand security pain points, security friction (minimizing it and, in some circumstances, introducing it) and team workflow—essentially how security affects productivity. In my opinion, these are the only real metrics that matter.

This piece of work will also highlight current attitudes and behaviours towards security as well as blind spots and ways of working. The data that this provides helps to establish a baseline for your environment, which can be used to develop and plan interventions that are actually contextually relevant, be they administrative or technology based. Ultimately, the environment needs to facilitate the change that it wants; otherwise, you're doing busy work.

What Actions Can Be Taken to Direct Cultural Change?

First and foremost, senior leadership support is key, but on a practical level you need to have staff that lead and manage the operational, tactical, and strategic work.

In addition to a security culture study, establishing a security champions network is a key initiative. Essentially, volunteer staff who help to raise awareness of key security messages, scale your security efforts, and provide vital feedback of how things actually work on the ground. They become people within their teams/business area that colleagues can come to for guidance and direction.

Is There a Success or Horror Story You'd Like to Share Related to Culture Change?

I have seen particularly bad approaches where a blame culture existed with a very obvious distrust of the security function. However, it's not always that bad, as I've also come across companies that have had little resource but have clearly defined their outcomes and taken a slow but steady path that led to genuine and positive security changes. The key here was that they listened to the needs of the business rather than try to do what they thought was needed.

How Does a Culture Evolve (or How Often)?

In my experience, it depends on a number of things:

- The sector
- The size of the organization
- The actual risks it faces
- If it's previously been the victim of a breach

Typically, if an organization has been the victim of a breach, experience shows that that can be a catalyst for change (though not always); or, if a competitor has been breached, that can also be the impetus for change—a case of "we don't want that to happen to us."

The important thing to remember is that there are always varying levels of evolution, so it's more prudent to accept and understand that you make the best of resources at hand.

Chapter 15
Parting Thoughts

And suddenly you know: It's time to start something new and trust the magic of beginnings.

Meister Eckhart

Well, you made it! While this may be the end of this book, it is only the beginning of your security culture journey. We hope you've been encouraged by the fact that security culture doesn't have to be a mysterious topic. We also hope you've been inspired by many of the experiences and thoughts conveyed in our expert interviews. In all of this, we see that, yes, security culture is wrapped up in the intricacies of human nature and social dynamics, but it is also something that can be defined, measured, and—most importantly—influenced.

Wondering where to go from here? If so, we suggest the next steps:

1. Engage the community.
2. Be a lifelong learner.
3. Be a realistic optimist.

Engage the Community

The power of community and collaboration cannot be overstated. They not only help fuel new ideas and continued encouragement, but members within the community will undoubtedly serve as sounding boards and people who will help you identify your blind spots. Make it a priority to get involved in communities that will support and challenge you.

One such community is waiting for you on LinkedIn right now. This group can help support discussion, idea sharing, and group problem-solving; just search "Security Culture Community" on LinkedIn (or go to www.linkedin.com/groups/8707418). We look forward to seeing you there!

We also recommend the following communities:

- **The International Association of Security Awareness Professionals (IASAP):** The IASAP is a members-only organization comprising security awareness professionals interested in sharing best practices, challenging each other, and pushing the industry forward. They have monthly webinars, three in-person meetings annually, and a private online community for year-round connections with resources, member question-and-answer sessions, and event recordings. Go to https://iasap-group.org for details.
- **KB4-CON:** KB4-CON is KnowBe4's annual user conference. There is content for everyone from CISOs to full-time security awareness and culture program managers to IT admins with 15 other fires to put out. With keynotes, breakout sessions, and workshops, there is something for everyone. Keynotes sessions always include live hacking demonstrations, KnowBe4 executives providing insight about how best to use the KnowBe4 platform, what the future holds, industry luminaries, and other speakers with interesting and insightful messages. Go to www.knowbe4.com/kb4-con for more information.
- **National Cybersecurity Alliance:** The National Cybersecurity Alliance is the organization that birthed Cybersecurity

Awareness Month. They focus on building strong public/private partnerships to create and implement broad-reaching education and awareness efforts to empower users at home, work, and school with the information they need to keep themselves, their organizations, their systems, and their sensitive information safe and secure online and encourage a culture of cybersecurity. This group actively seeks to engage and equip the security awareness and culture community through webinars and in-person events. See https://staysafeonline.org.

- **SANS Security Awareness Summits:** Each year, SANS holds security awareness summits in both North America and Europe. These are vendor-neutral, community-driven events with agendas focused on program management, metrics, user engagement, and more. You can find information at https://sans.org/SecAwareSummit.

Be sure to check out the companion website for this book. We'll post periodic updates, new research, interesting new tidbits, as well as links to any industry conferences/events we hear of that touch on security culture. Head over to https://SecurityCultureBook.com.

Be a Lifelong Learner

One of the biggest points we hope you take from this book is that security culture isn't about security—it's about people. And it's about the interpersonal dynamics that shape communities. The cybersecurity part is just an overlay on top of those other dynamics. In other words, your path to build a security culture that will be a true asset to your organization requires a genuine understanding of—and interest in—the human side of the cybersecurity equation.

Become a student of the social sciences, of human nature, and seek out books, podcasts, and communities that help broaden that interest. You never know when inspiration and insight will strike, but you can up the frequency of these by cultivating a lifestyle of continually digging into new and different fields of study.

Certifications for Security Awareness and Culture Professionals

If you are looking to hire (or become) someone who has a demonstrated level of knowledge and understanding regarding the intricacies of security awareness and culture, then we'd recommend starting with the Security Awareness and Culture Professional (SACP) certification. Launched in 2021, this vendor-neutral certification covers a wide range of topics related to awareness, behavior management, and influencing security culture. This credential was created by H-Layer Credentialing. You can find more information at www.thehlayer.com.

You may also be interested in the Sans Security Awareness Professional (SSAP) credential. Students can test for this certification upon completion of the two-day SANS *MGT433: Managing Human Risk: Mature Security Awareness Programs* course. More information is available at www.sans.org/security-awareness-training/career-development/credential.

Be a Realistic Optimist

Every journey starts with a first step. Some of the ideas and goals expressed in the previous chapters may seem difficult to achieve; almost all of them require you to rely on other people in your organization. You'll need to *sell* many of the ideas up, down, and across your organization. And, as you've seen, this is about building maturity through an iterative process. That means that there are several aspects of your security culture journey that require time and consistency to reach their full potential. Rest assured, however, there are some short-term wins to be had, such as phishing training, seeing initial culture measurements, and more.

Always remember your purpose. As someone with responsibility for managing risk in your organization, you are ultimately serving the very people you are seeking to influence. The only way to change them is to have empathy and appreciate who they are and why they struggle. Only then will you be able to find the best method(s) to drive change. The best leaders work from a sense of passion that comes from knowing that they are serving a grand cause. Here's yours: to help build a safer and more secure world, one person, one organization, one family, and one community at a time.

Conclusion

We hope you've enjoyed reading this book as much as we've enjoyed writing it for you. We truly believe that the next few years will be critical within the cybersecurity community. These years will be when the community begins to gain a firm grasp on what security culture really is and how it can be influenced. This will help create greater empathy and greater insights and usher in a much-needed evolution in our understanding of how we can and should manage human risk. Welcome to the security culture re-evolution.

Welcome to the security culture re-evolution.

Keep in touch. We'd love to hear your stories or be able to help in any way that we can. If you've enjoyed this book and found it helpful, please recommend it to others within your network.

You can easily connect with us on LinkedIn, Twitter, or via the accompanying website for this book. Here are the links:

- Perry's social links:
  - LinkedIn /in/perrycarpenter
  - Twitter @perrycarpenter

- Kai's social links:
  - LinkedIn: `/in/kairoer`
  - Twitter `@KaiRoerNO`
- Companion website for *The Security Culture Playbook*: `https://SecurityCultureBook.com`

All the best!
Perry Carpenter & Kai Roer
February, 2022

Bibliography

Betsy U., Nurse, J., Bada, M., and Furnell, S. (2021). Developing a cyber security culture: Current practices and future needs. *Computers and Security Journal.*

@bjfogg. (March 31, 2011). 3 truths about human nature: We're lazy, social, and creatures of habit. Design products for this reality (accessed 28 January 2021). https://twitter.com/bjfogg/status/53486588944056321?lang=en

Braue, D. (2021). Global ransomware damage costs predicted to exceed $265 billion by 2031. *Cybercrime Magazine.* https://cybersecurityventures.com/global-ransomware-damage-costs-predicted-to-reach-250-billion-usd-by-2031

Buss, M. (2017). Why you should be a culture carrier. Granify. https://medium.com/granify/why-you-should-be-a-culture-carrier-e8ed0dfba6ce

Carpenter, P. (2019). *Transformational Security Awareness: What Neuroscientists, Storytellers, and Marketers Can Teach Us About Driving Secure Behaviors.* Wiley, 22–23.

Chai, W. Confidentiality, integrity and availability (CIA triad). WhatIs.com. Updated 2021. https://whatis.techtarget.com/definition/Confidentiality-integrity-and-availability-CIA

Childress, J. (2017). *Culture Rules!: The 10 Core Principles of Corporate Culture and How to Use Them to Create Greater Business Success.* Principia Associates.

CMMI Institute Resource Center. DMM Model At-A-Glance. CMMI Institute (2019). https://stage.cmmiinstitute.com/resource-files/public/dmm-model-at-a-glance

Da Veiga, A., & Eloff, J.H.P. A framework and assessment instrument for information security culture. *Computers & Security.* 2010; 29: 196–207.

Dunn, S. (2014). Managing human error in maintenance. Assetivity. www.assetivity.com.au/articles/reliability-improvement/managing-human-error-in-maintenance

Eriksen, A-C., Petrič, G., and Roer, K. (2021). Security culture and credential sharing: How improved security culture reduces credential sharing in cybersecurity. www.knowbe4.com/hubfs/Security%20Culture%20and%20Credential%20Sharing.pdf

Fogg, B. J. Fogg Behavior Model (accessed 25 January 2021). https://behaviormodel.org

Fogg, B. J. (2020). *Tiny Habits: The Small Changes That Change Everything.* Houghton Mifflin Harcourt.

Fung, B. and Sands, G. (2021). Ransomware attackers used compromised password to access Colonial Pipeline. CNN. www.cnn.com/2021/06/04/politics/colonial-pipeline-ransomware-attack-password/index.html

Hameed, M. and Arachchilage, N. (2021). The role of self-efficacy on the adoption of information systems security innovations: A meta-analysis assessment. Personal and Ubiquitous Computing; 25. https://doi.org/10.1007/s00779-021-01560-1

Hill, K. (2021). The Kaseya ransomware attack: A timeline. CSO. www.csoonline.com/article/3626703/the-kaseya-ransomware-attack-a-timeline.html

IBM. (2021). How much does a data breach cost? www.ibm.com/security/data-breach

Institute for Cybersecurity & Digital Trust. (2022). Cybersecurity Canon. Ohio State University. https://icdt.osu.edu/cybercanon

International Data Corporation. (2021). IDC survey finds more than one third of organizations worldwide have experienced a ransomware attack or breach. www.idc.com/getdoc.jsp?containerId=prUS48159121

Internet Security Alliance. (2020). NCAD Director's Handbook on Cyber-Risk Oversight. www.nacdonline.org/insights/publications.cfm?ItemNumber=67298

Kahneman, D. (2013). *Thinking, Fast and Slow.* Farrar, Straus and Giroux.

Khan, B., et al. (2011). Effectiveness of information security methods based on psychological theories. *African Journal of Business Management*; 5(26).

KnowBe4. (2020). The Rise of Security Culture. https://info.knowbe4.com/rise-of-security-culture

KnowBe4. Security Culture Survey (SCS). Updated 2022. https://support.knowbe4.com/hc/en-us/articles/360037393134-What-Is-the-Security-Culture-Survey-SCS-

Lundy O, & Cowling A. *Strategic Human Resource Management*. Routledge; 1996.

Martens, B. 11 Facts + stats on smishing (SMS phishing) in 2022. *SafetyDetectives* (accessed 29 January 2021). www.safetydetectives.com/blog/what-is-smishing-sms-phishing-facts

Meyer, Erin. (2016). *The Culture Map*. PublicAffairs.

Petrič, G. and Roer, K. (2022). The impact of formal and informal organizational norms on susceptibility to phishing: Combining survey and field experiment data. *Telematics and Informatics*; 67. www.sciencedirect.com/science/article/pii/S0736585321002057

Phishlabs. (2021). Quarterly threat trends & intelligence. https://info.phishlabs.com/quarterly-threat-trends-and-intelligence-november-2021

Pollini, A., et al. (2021). Leveraging human factors in cybersecurity: An integrated methodological approach. *Cognition, Technology & Work*. https://doi.org/10.1007/s10111-021-00683-y

Register. The ransomware has gone nuclear (accessed 27 January 2021). https://whitepapers.theregister.com/paper/view/8722/ransomware-has-gone-nuclear

Reuters. (2021). Meatpacker JBS says it paid equivalent of $11 mln in ransomware attack. www.reuters.com/technology/jbs-paid-11-mln-response-ransomware-attack-2021-06-09

Roberts, S. A. (2021). *Exploring the Relationships Between User Cybersecurity Knowledge, Cybersecurity and Cybercrime Attitudes, and Online Risky Behaviors*. Dissertation. Northcentral University.

Schneier, B. (2000). *Secrets and Lies: Digital Security in a Networked World*. Wiley.

Seals, T. (2021). Ransomware volumes hit record highs as 2021 wears on. *Threat Post*. https://threatpost.com/ransomware-volumes-record-highs-2021/168327

Sheridan, K. (2021). 85% of data breaches involve human interaction: Verizon DBIR. *Dark Reading*. www.darkreading.com/operations/85--of-data-breaches-involve-human-interaction-verizon-dbir/d/d-id/1341012

Sjouwerman, S. (2021). The latest ransomware attacks can require a data breach notification. KnowBe4. https://blog.knowbe4.com/the-latest-ransomware-attacks-can-require-a-data-breach-notification

Stewart, G. and Lacey, D. (2012). Death by a Thousand Facts: Criticising the Technocratic Approach to Information Security Awareness. *Inf. Manag. Comput. Secur.* 20(1).

Thaler, R. H. (2015). *Misbehaving: The Making of Behavioral Economics.* W. W. Norton & Co.

Thaler, R. H. and Sunstein, C. R. (2009). *Nudge: Improving Decisions About Health, Wealth, and Happiness.* Penguin Books.

Uchendu, B, et al. (2021). Developing a cyber security culture: Current practices and future needs. *Computers & Security;* 109.

Verizon. 2021 Data Breach Investigations Report. www.verizon.com/business/resources/reports/dbir

Index